Preaching the New Millennium

Preaching the New Millennium

John Killinger

Abingdon Press
Nashville

This book is printed on elemental-chlorine–free paper.

Library of Congress Cataloging-in-Publication Data

Killinger, John.
    Preaching the new millennium/John Killinger.
       p.   cm.
    Includes bibliographical references.
    ISBN 0-687-08737-6 (paper: adhesive-bound)
       1. Millennium.   2. Two thousand, A.D.—Sermons.   3. Sermons,
American.   4. Preaching.   I. Title.
    BT891.K55   1999
    251—dc21   98-39715
                                                                    CIP

Scripture quotations, unless otherwise indicated, are from the New Revised Standard Version Bible, copyright © 1989, by the Division of Christian Education of the National Council of the Churches of Christ in the United States of America.

99 00 01 02 03 04 05 06 07 08—10 9 8 7 6 5 4 3

MANUFACTURED IN THE UNITED STATES OF AMERICA

This book
is cheerfully dedicated
to our dear friends at

The Little Stone Church

on Mackinac Island, Michigan,

which this year celebrates
one hundred years
of service
in one of the most beautiful spots
on earth!

Contents

Introduction

R ising to the occasion." It's a phrase we sometimes use. It implies that we can summon the strength or wisdom from somewhere to make ourselves equal to something that is happening.

But what is perhaps not implicit in the phrase is the fact that occasions themselves contribute something to our rising. That is, they often elicit from us the most we have to give. They trigger our adrenaline supply and suddenly we find ourselves rising above even the best we would normally do.

It happens to players on the athletic field, musicians giving concerts, soldiers in wartime, actors on the stage, chefs preparing important dinners, teachers giving lectures, salespersons in the act of selling, poets writing poems, surgeons performing difficult operations.

And it happens to preachers. Preachers often preach their best sermons on special occasions.

John of Antioch, the preacher known as Chrysostom, the "Golden Mouth," did. This brilliant fourth-century preacher was already vastly popular in the ancient city of Antioch. But he did his most memorable preaching during several weeks when the Antiochenes were afraid for their lives. A mob had become angry over taxes and defaced the statues of Emperor Theodosius, his wife, and their two sons. Then the citizens realized that when the emperor heard about it he might well send his army to destroy the town and put everyone to a horrible death. Anxiously, they sent Bishop Flavian off to Constantinople to plead for clemency. During the interval of several weeks, as the citizens waited in hand-wringing suspense, Chrysostom preached his famous series of twenty-one homilies "On the Statues," urging people to take refuge in their heavenly Ruler. Those who heard these sermons said they were among the very finest the golden-toned preacher ever preached.

Odo of Cluny, who became Pope Urban II, preached his greatest sermon in 1095 after receiving word from the patriarch of Constantinople that the Seljuk Turks were at the gates of his city, the seat of Eastern Christianity. Assembling as many churchmen as he could rouse to a council in Clermont, France, Urban preached a fiery sermon denouncing the infidels and calling for an immediate response of force. The result was the first crusade, the beginning of a series of efforts to retake the East, and particularly the Holy Land, that would change the face and culture of medieval Europe.

The great preaching friars of the Franciscan and Dominican orders in the thirteenth century rose to preach against the general corruption that had fallen on the church during the Middle Ages and excelled at bringing fresh truth to people in the local vernacular, thus stimulating new growth and devotion in every country they visited.

Luther and Zwingli and Calvin were occasional preachers, often rising to their greatest heights when dealing with fierce opposition to the Reformation movement. And Zwingli preached some of his finest sermons in 1519, when a plague broke out in the city of Zurich. He was away from the city when it happened, but rushed back to take his place among his flock and comfort them with sermons on Christ and the afterlife.

John Wesley's best known and possibly most outstanding sermon was one called "The Great Assize," which he preached in 1758 in Bedford, England, as the people were gathering for the assizes to be presided over by Sir Edward

Clive. His text, "We shall all stand before the judgment seat of Christ" (Romans 14:10 KJV), must have struck a resonant note with all who had business before the court.

The greatest sermon delivered by Arthur John Gossip, one of the most eloquent Scottish preachers of this century, was, declared his congregation without hesitation, the one he gave immediately following the death of his wife. It was called "But When Life Tumbles In, What Then?" It was said that there was not a dry eye in the church, and many people went out to change their lives after hearing Gossip's noble words.

The most electrifying sermon I ever heard from one of my pastors was the one he preached following the assassination of President John F. Kennedy. Normally a very staid and even boring preacher, he rose to the occasion to preach an insightful and encouraging sermon to a congregation still in shock and disbelief. And his was not the only eloquent response to the assassination. Subsequent collections of sermons about it revealed that the murder of the president had had a similar effect all over the country, challenging many ministers to make eloquent responses.

The same phenomenon occurred again following the deaths of Martin Luther King, Jr., and Robert Kennedy, after the bombing of the Murrah Federal Building in Oklahoma City, and after the death of Princess Diana of England. Preachers who are usually weak and uninspiring speakers are often galvanized by events that have disturbed wide segments of the populace, so that they mount their pulpits and say powerful and memorable things to their people.

Even certain occasions of the church year—especially Christmas and Easter—appear to bring out the best in some preachers. Congregations are excited about the occasions. They are talking about them and preparing for them in their families. There is a general air of expectancy and anticipation. The preachers, caught up in the preparation and excitement, find themselves unusually stimulated and eager to preach on their subjects. They rise to the occasion. The occasion buoys them, lifts them, gives unexpected amplitude to their words. And the sermons, say their parishioners, are among their very best.

We are now facing one of the greatest occasions of our lifetime: the approach of a new millennium. Only a small percentage of the earth's population ever gets to live from one millennium into another. It is a rare and special privilege. People will grow more and more feverish about it as the moment approaches. It will be a fantastic opportunity for preaching! Unlike some great occasions, this one will be protracted. People are already beginning to think about it and plan for it. Not only that, but the newness of the experience of entering another millennium will linger for several months after the actual date has passed. This means that the wise preacher will rise to the occasion not just once but many times during the period of transition. His or her sermons about the new millennium should find unusual resonance in people's hearts and minds again and again.

This book was written to help you in your thinking and understanding of this extraordinary phenomenon. It will not produce your great sermons for you. But it will provide a stimulus for thinking about the transition from one millennium to another and help you to focus on the phenomenon. It will also assist you in assessing the mood of your people during the transition months and in reflecting on the ways in which you can appropriately and honestly take advantage of that mood to do some of your best preaching ever.

One thing is certain. If you are not a good preacher during the waning months of the old millennium and the first months of the new one, you never will be. This is the best opportunity—or at least the most prolonged—you will ever have!

JOHN KILLINGER

The End of the First Millennium

As the end of the second millennium since Christ fast approaches, it's helpful to ask a question: What was the end of the first millennium like? How did people react as they faced the approach of the second millennium, the one we are now finishing?

According to the journal of Radulph (also Ralph or Raoul) Glaber, a bald-headed monk (we know he was bald because "Glaber" meant "baldpate") attached to the monasteries of Dijon and Cluny in France during the first half of the eleventh century, there were dramatic reactions all over Britain and Europe. January 1, 1000, was expected to be the great Day of Wrath promised in the Scriptures, when God would pour out storms and plagues on the earth and people would be caught up in the air to be judged before the great assizes of the Lord for all their sins and wickedness. Accordingly many people spent the latter half of the year 999 giving away their property, or selling it and giving the proceeds to the poor, hoping to avert condemnation of the sort mentioned again and again in the Gospels for those who failed to feed the hungry and care for the homeless.

Some people in France claimed to see the skies cloven by a great bolt of lightning and then to see a mighty dragon in place of the lightning, breathing out flames and destruction for the human race. A group of villagers in England said there was blood in the rain that fell on their streets and fields. Others, in Italy, Germany, and Bohemia, reported seeing great armies clashing in the skies overhead. Mt. Vesuvius in Italy spewed forth flames and sulfur several times as the millennium approached, and occasionally hurled sizable stones for great distances, warning of the wrath to come. "Almost all the cities of Italy and Gaul," declared Glaber, "were ravaged by flames." Once even St. Peter's basilica in Rome, the very center of Western Christendom, burst suddenly into flames; but when thousands of people rushed inside and began loudly confessing their sins the fire immediately abated.

There was a sudden flurry of church-building all over the world, said Glaber, as though the world "were clothing herself everywhere in a white garment of churches." The cry on everyone's tongue was *Veni, domine Jesu*—"Come, Lord Jesus"—for they believed it would all be over at the stroke of midnight on December 31, 999.

Hordes of pilgrims from around the globe descended on Jerusalem, then still a relatively small city, expecting that the Lord would return there to reign over the world. "On the threshold of the aforesaid thousandth year," wrote Glaber, "so innumerable a multitude began to flock from all parts of the world to the sepulchre of our Savior at Jerusalem, as no man could before have expected.... For many purposed and wished to die in the Holy City." The streets of the city and the roads for miles around Jerusalem were clogged by travelers, and the Church of the Holy Sepulchre, which was to play such a large part in the Crusades in coming centuries, was thronged to the point of bursting, with people hanging from the rafters and the window ledges, wanting to be present at this shrine of devotion when the Lord returned.

When Pope Sylvester II sang the midnight mass at St. Peter's in the hour approaching midnight on the last day of the old millennium, the church, the great square before it, and the streets surrounding them both were packed with worshipers. Despite the great crowd, many people inside the church and out threw themselves on the ground, their arms spread wide so that their bodies made the shape of the cross, and waited in prayer and panic for the final words of the mass, *Ite, missa est*, and the tolling of the great bell above them. Some people died of fright, reported Glaber in his diary, and others were severely stricken by strokes and heart attacks.

At last the words were spoken and the bell began to toll. Soon the bells were tolling all over the city, as indeed they were in many parts of Christendom. People waited in breathless silence. When the tolling continued and nothing happened, they began to look around in astonishment. Some laughed, some cried. Soon they were dancing and shouting and hugging one another, and the crowds erupted into a bedlam of rejoicing.

The earth had been spared. Christ had not returned at all.

The Sober Truth

It was a beautiful story, and a very credible one. People believed it for centuries. After all, Glaber was a man of the cloth. Not only that, but in 1605 Cardinal Baronius, librarian to the Vatican, quoted Glaber's account in his *Ecclesiastical Annals*, adding his own imprimatur to the story. Over a century later, a prominent Scottish historian, a Protestant named William Robertson (1721–1793), republished the account and gave it even wider circulation. And a century after that, the great French historian Jules Michelet (1798–1874) likewise retold and endorsed it. By this time it was taken as the gospel truth.

But not by everyone. In 1873, a devout and scholarly Benedictine, François Plaine, announced that Glaber's story was a fake and a fraud. People in his own time paid little attention to Glaber, Plaine showed, for he was a drinker and a blowhard who bounced around from monastery to monastery (which in those days were often little more than inns for travelers), tipping his glass and telling tales for the amusement of his friends. The responsible clergy of the time, said Plaine, actually discouraged people from being afraid at the approach of a new millennium, and downplayed the possibility of Christ's return.

Early in the twentieth century, a renowned historian named George Lincoln Burr published an article in *The American Historical Review* summarizing the history of Glaber's account and branding it as nothing more than a myth or a legend concocted by the imaginative friar himself. What we forget, said Burr, is that few people in that day were even aware of the date. The Christian calendar as we know it had been adopted by Pope John XIII scarcely thirty years before the end of the millennium, and it was seldom used outside of Rome until well into the eleventh century. Most people could not read and write or understand ciphers, and counted their lives only from sun-up to sun-down and liturgical holiday to liturgical holiday, not from year to year. "To us who are stared at by calendars and date-lines," said Burr, "who must every day of our lives again and again write day and month and year, it is not easy to realize a world wherein all this is the affair of priests and notaries."[1]

To be fair, there probably were some people who were concerned about the end of the millennium and expected that Christ might return at the stroke of midnight. Yet even they were surely comforted by Christ's warning that "about that day and hour no one knows, neither the angels of heaven, nor the Son, but only the Father" (Matthew 24:36). It is likely that people then approached the turning of the millennia much as we do today, as a time for taking stock of their lives and deciding how they would live in the new era, and not with an undue concern that the world would suddenly be shaken by an eschatological confrontation.

What the World Was Like Then

When we reflect on it, we are struck by the fact that there exist no real data about the end of the first millennium—only Radulph Glaber's fanciful and erroneous report. What a contrast with the end of our own millennium, which is being voluminously chronicled by videotape, computer records, newspapers, and books of every kind!

We are reminded of what a simple, benighted world people then inhabited, when few historians bothered to record major events and the records of those who did were usually lost by fire, mildew, and general neglect. The centuries from approximately 600 C.E. to 1000 C.E. are often called the Dark Ages, not only because it was a period of ignorance and superstition in most of Europe but also because we know so little about them. We are simply "in the dark" about them, and are forced to deduce much of what we know from the scant records that do exist.

It is easy to guess that the period leading up to the year 1000 was a time of constant struggle and warfare for most of the people of Europe and Britain. The barbarians were pounding at the edges of the Roman Empire for almost two centuries before Rome finally collapsed in 476 C.E. These same warlike tribes, who often destroyed learning and records in their wake, swept up across Europe and down into Britain for another two centuries. Then the Moors, who had become aggressive and well-organized, overran North Africa and parts of Southern Europe. They were finally halted at the Battle of Tours in 732, but not before leaving their own mark on the architectures and cultures of the areas they conquered.

The Germanic nations, largely descended from the Indo-European tribes that had destroyed Rome, had become aligned and powerful by the tenth century, and were generally regarded as the force to be reckoned with in Europe. The Italian republics, led particularly by Venice, were the foremost trading peoples and masters of the Mediterranean. The French and Spanish kingdoms were also relatively strong, partly as a result of having been instrumental in stopping the Moors and partly because of the brilliant leadership of Charlemagne, who became Holy Roman Emperor in 800 and revived memories of the empire's greatness. Britain, being insular, appears not to have figured prominently in the history of the time. Alfred, who died in 900, was the first notable king of England, and the country remained largely divided and depleted by the constant attacks of the Vikings from Norway and Denmark, who had been pillaging Britain since 787 and occupied large portions of it in the tenth century.

Christianity, on the other hand, continued to establish itself as the principal religion of both Britain and Europe, with missionaries abounding in spite of the low state of learning. Part of this missionary effort grew out of the efforts of the monastery at Cluny, which energetically campaigned for reform of priests and monks, demanding clerical celibacy and putting an end to the practice of simony (selling benefices) and lay investiture of prelates. When Abbot Odilo of Cluny died in 1048, the mother-house had established 63 monasteries across Europe and Britain. By 1000 even Hungary, Bohemia, and the Scandinavian countries had been Christianized, and in the year 1000 the Norwegian settlers of Iceland decided at their annual assembly, the Althing, to accept the Christian way. Vladimir I of Russia married a Byzantine princess and adopted the Greek Orthodox form of Christianity, which continues today to be the primary religion of the Russian peoples.

The social structure of the times was generally feudalistic. That is, it was based on the understanding that the king had a divine right to the land he controlled, and that he was authorized in turn to delegate barons or knights to serve under him, for which service they received supervision of manorial estates, many of which amounted to duchies or small countries. The barons also sublet the land to vassals who pledged to be faithful to them, and the vassals owned or controlled serfs or peasant people who actually did the majority of the work on the land and in the villages. In case of war, the king called on his barons who in turn called on his vassals and their peasants as willing combatants in the king's cause. Roughly a third of all cultivated land was set aside by the vassals for their lords or barons, and the barons were expected to pay fees or taxes to their kings in addition to being ready to fight for them.

By the year 1000, there appears to have been a system of courtly rules in effect to govern the behavior of knights and their servants all over Britain and Europe. It put great emphasis on honorable behavior, and as a heightened devotion to Mary began to permeate society during the eleventh and twelfth centuries, on courtly love as well, whereby knights performed their courageous service for the love of highborn ladies.

No one is sure how extensive it was, but it is believed that a sizable part of the population belonged to a free merchant class that existed alongside the feudal classes. These individuals were traders, manufacturers, and sellers, serving necessary functions in society in both war and peacetime.

Almost all the industry of the time centered on either war or agriculture. Every woman, even those who were highborn, was taught to spin, weave, sew, and stitch, and was continually engaged in making cloth and clothing. James Westfall Thompson's *Economic and Social History of the Middle Ages* lists blacksmiths, wheelwrights, saddlers, shoemakers, soap makers, beer brewers, wine makers, net makers, carpenters, wood turners, shield and armament makers, tanners, carvers, fullers, and coopers among the artisans on both lay and ecclesial manors. Some branches of industry, such as mills, beer breweries, winepresses, and salt works, required extensive organization and factory-like management. As salt was considered so essential a part of the economy, all salt works belonged directly to the king, even though they were operated by his vassals.

The German nations were the preeminent miners and metalworkers of the time, which is one reason they were considered so formidable in battle. The Italians were especially noted for their trading networks, which extended even as far as the Orient. The French were already noted as the best wine makers of Europe.

In short, the Western world at the turn of the second millennium was largely in a state of ferment and change. The old Roman Empire had disintegrated, and with it most of the culture of the ancient world. In its place there were hundreds of minor nations, many drawn into alliances with other nations by linguistic or family relationships. Latin, which had been the language of the empire, had largely disappeared except as the official language of the church, and new languages were emerging everywhere. An abysmal ignorance prevailed in most countries. Schooling was emphasized in many of the monasteries and a few of the royal courts, but otherwise there was no education at all except in the ways of trade and warfare. Even the parish clergy were often ignorant and untutored, and superstition prevailed over philosophy and theology in many of their lives. It had in many ways been generally a dark and ignoble period in the history of the world.

The Contrast of the Present Situation

This extremely brief reminder of the conditions of Europe at the beginning of the present millennium is intended to emphasize how far our world has come in only a thousand years. When we think of the major events that transpired since the year 1000—the discovery and development of the Americas, the virtual abandonment of monarchy in favor of democracy, the insurgence in the church that produced the Protestant movement, the rise of modern science, the triumphs of the industrial revolution, the development of modern education, the splitting of the atom, the beginnings of space travel, the growth of communications—we cannot but be impressed or even shocked by the astounding changes that have occurred. Our lives have been so transformed from those of our ancestors only a few generations ago that they would be literally unrecognizable to them.

Now we stand on the verge of a new period of time commensurate with that one. What will the new era bring forth? What will be its major achievements, the hallmarks by which successive millennia will remember it? Who will human beings become in the thousand years that lie before us? With global warming and a thinning ozone layer threatening our ecology and more and more nations developing nuclear and biological weapons capable of wiping out the entire race, will we even *survive* another millennium?

These are all sobering questions. As ministers, we cannot afford to ignore them. They should become part of our daily thinking in the months and years ahead. They should find their way into our sermons and devotionals, so that our congregants face them with us.

Unfortunately we don't have a single sermon preached by a minister on the eve of the year 1000 C.E. Recording methods then were very inefficient, and any written sermons from that date have simply disappeared, destroyed by fire or flood or the inevitable neglect that overtakes most sermons.

What would the sermons of the day have said, had they been preserved? That life is short and the future unpredictable? That a new millennium is a good time to renew our commitment to God by examining our consciences, confessing our sins, and vowing to be more devoted followers of Christ? That God is gracious to have spared the world for the start of another millennium?

Perhaps.

But given the rather recent introduction of the Christian calendar and the slowness with which the world changed in those days, it is rather unlikely that sermons then would have said much at all, if anything, about the end of one age and the beginning of another. In all probability, the clergy then were relatively insensitive to such an epochal moment. We know that many of them, being ignorant and unlearned, merely read their homilies from a book known as a *homiliary*, a collection prepared for just such a purpose. And the homiliaries were rarely if ever designed to address a particular occasion.

We would judge that a significant opportunity lost, for we know that particular occasions are often the most listenable moments congregations have. They are the times when the mind is open and the heart is receptive to the truths of the gospel in ways they seldom are.

The big question then is about how *we* are going to respond to the opportunity of speaking to people on the eve of *our* new millennium. No one ever gets a chance to preach more than once at the turn of a century. And even fewer preachers ever get an opportunity to preach at the turn of a millennium. It is a rare, almost unparalleled experience, one we dare not miss.

This book's *raison d'être* is to help sharpen our perception of this experience, to prepare our thinking for the event itself, so that we aren't merely lost in the usual programming miasma and don't miss it during the weeks and months when we could most enjoy and treat it with advantage. In the following chapter we'll look at the responses some people have already voiced to the approach of the end of the millennium. Perhaps that will enable us to get our own psyches more in tune for it. Then we'll survey some of the more potent images and metaphors in the Bible for preaching more directly about the new millennium and its possibilities for our lives in particular and human culture in general. In another chapter we'll deal with the topic of the minister's spirituality and how it is affected by the approach of a new age. And finally we'll look at some sermons crafted with an eye toward the turning of the millennium—suggestions of the kind of preaching you may want to do for your congregation.

It's too bad Ralph the Bald isn't around today to chronicle the end of *this* millennium. He might have a lot more to write about.

Popular Emotions
as the
Millennium Approaches

Some people are prematurely high on millennial spirit. Major resorts and hotels around the world are already booked for New Year's Eve at the end of the old millennium. The Concorde planes are reserved for gala excursions that will whisk passengers from time zone to time zone faster than the speed of sound, so that they will experience celebrations in several of the world's great cities as they circumnavigate the globe. The New Year's Eve 1999 party lists at prominent restaurants and theaters in Paris, London, New York, Los Angeles, and Tokyo were finalized as early as a year and a half in advance, and open reservations are being held only for the rich and famous. Most politicians, socialites, and futurists can already tell you where they will be as the ball drops in Times Square and the third millennium after Christ makes its debut.

According to William Ecenbarger, there is a new line of skin-care products with the name Millenium (note the misspelling), Farberware is marketing a nonstick cookware

called Farberware Millennium, and the Chrysler Corporation has named one of its cars the Millennium. The Millennium Society, a six-thousand-member group that commenced planning in 1979, intends to stage twenty-four spectacles, one for each time zone, as midnight on New Year's Eve 1999 occurs in each zone. Among other places, there are celebrations planned for the Great Wall of China, the Taj Mahal, Mount Fuji, the Eiffel Tower—and Times Square, of course.[1]

The English government is building a controversial Millennium Dome on the south bank of the River Thames. The London *Times* reports that talks are going on between Buckingham Palace and Number 10 Downing Street about the celebration on December 31, 1999. According to one plan, Queen Elizabeth and Prime Minister Tony Blair will sail down the Thames from Westminster to St. Paul's for a church service, then proceed to the Maritime Museum in Greenwich. There, at precisely midnight, a laser beam will be fired along the Greenwich meridian encircling the globe. The queen will then perform the opening ceremony for the dome.

Time magazine reports that Robert Halmi, who is producing a millennial extravaganza for ABC television, has asked some of America's leading playwrights—Larry Gilbart, John Guare, David Mamet, Steve Martin, Elaine May, Terrence McNally, Arthur Miller, Neil Simon, Wendy Wasserstein, and August Wilson—to provide ABC with teleplays about the millennium. All ten plays are scheduled to be aired during the November 1999 sweeps week.[2]

By the time we reach the end of the year before the new century, the constant publicity in newspapers, magazines, and television programming will have made everybody in the world—even in developing countries in Africa, Asia, and South and Central America—hyperconscious of the beginning of the new millennium. Patrons in nightclubs, gamblers in casinos, worshipers in mosques and churches, clerks in the marketplaces, attendees at sports events, patients in hospitals, and children playing in the streets will all be affected by millennial fever. The passing of a millennium, which happens only once every thousand years, will be a topic of conversation for talk show hosts, stand-up comedians, news commentators, magazine editors, teachers, and preachers everywhere. The subject will be unavoidable. There will be more comments made about it than there were about the death of Princess Diana, the trial of O. J. Simpson, or President Clinton's affair with Monica Lewinsky. The very air of the planet will be saturated with talk about it. It will be on literally every person's mind.

Some people will of course feign indifference. They will choose not to be caught in the sweep toward millennial interest, the way they resist being drawn into any popular trend. Brian E. Daley, professor of theology at the University of Notre Dame, near the end of a long article about apocalypticism from St. Augustine to the present, says, "Most of us, on that New Year's Eve, will probably note the passing of the century with mild interest, toast the new with a glass or two of bad champagne, and go to bed."[3]

Two retired teacher friends, Clayton and Anna Timmons, wrote: "Perhaps it's because we grew up in depression time, but our generation never thought of a bang-up celebration when we reached 21 or hit the fateful age of 40. So many of the younger set have already made exciting plans to cross over into the year 2000. We'll probably have a quiet gathering with friends and hope that all can stay awake until midnight."

Noted writer Ursula K. LeGuin, in an interview in *Parabola*, dismisses the crossover as a mere vanishing point. "What is it?" she says. "It's nothing. It's just another year, you know. The real year lies in its cyclicalness, in the seasons and in the movements of the earth among the stars, the solstices and the equinoxes. That, to me, is the reality of the

year. Then we attach numbers to these years, and one of them turns out to be the year one thousand. There's an arbitrariness to that number which I can't get away from."[4]

But even the people who show mild or little interest in the end of one millennium and beginning of another will surely be affected at unconscious levels by such a momentous event, and often more deeply than they suspect. The world community cannot pass through anything so significant as a millennial change without the influence being felt by every last one of its members.

Fear and Trepidation

There will be a sense of fearfulness among some as we glide through the century's end zone, just as Radulph Glaber said there was among people at the end of the first millennium after Christ. These persons may even feel that we are violating some kind of limit by going beyond the century in which we presently live, and that cosmic punishment must inevitably follow.

"I don't know if I want to live into the next millennium," one correspondent told me. "It would be like stepping onto the moon or entering the Holy of Holies. I don't feel worthy to live in another century, let alone another millennium. I feel as if I might combust and die."

Clair and Charlotte Berry, a couple living in Southern California, confess to a definite feeling of ambiguity about the approach of the new era. Clair says he looks forward with wonder to "continued space travel, instant global information, and further inroads on disease," but knows we will continue to live in "a contentious world filled with moral decline and spiritual poverty." Charlotte says: "It is all mind-boggling to me. The only thing that gives me hope is my assurance that God is dynamic and sufficient for every era and generation."

David Ernsburg, a psychiatrist, says that this feeling of unworthiness to enter a new millennium is more widespread than we generally realize. People who normally repress their guilt and live with it rather successfully become very aware of it when crossing some extremely important threshold such as marriage, ordination, or death. This is why such moments are sacralized by religious ordinances. The guilt then becomes sublimated into spiritual causality and is pardoned because it induces blessing. But there are no sacraments for translating entry into a new millennium and changing curse to blessing. Hence some persons fear the advent of the new millennium as the catalyst that will destroy them for their lack of holiness.

There is also the sense that a new millennium carries new opportunities and responsibilities, both of which induce fear and hesitance in certain people. As long as we were merely winding down at the end of an old millennium, these persons could drift with the tide and even find consolation in a sense of entropy, of everything's falling apart. But the opening of a new millennium carries for them a tremendous burden of possibility, one they would actually prefer to forswear.

The poet of this mood of entropic despair is surely Samuel Beckett, whose play *Waiting for Godot* is our classic statement of the winding down of everything. Two tramps, Didi and Gogo, wait around for the appearance of some character named Godot (critics have speculated that it may mean "little God"), whose coming, if it ever occurs, may start things up again. But if Godot ever comes, the tramps don't recognize him, and the play ends as it began, in a kind of measured torpor where everything—the tramps' lives, their dialogue, the weather, events in the world around them—appears to drift and drift without aim or purpose. One critic wrote that *Waiting for Godot* is "a play in which nothing happens—twice" because it is a play with two acts.

Martin Esslin pointed out in *The Theatre of the Absurd* that the first audience to really understand *Waiting for Godot* was one in Alcatraz prison. The inmates identified with waiting and drifting because there was nothing else they could do. They were caught in the same absurd reductionism of life that lies at the heart of the play. Most of them, like the two tramps, were powerless to effect any changes in society and the flow of history around them.

The elderly are often the members of society most likely to cherish the sense that things are petering out and to despair of things starting up again. Their own levels of personal energy are being depleted with the passing years, and they naturally begin to feel out of sync with new twists and turns in the social picture. Consequently there are probably more elderly folks than young persons who look with apprehension on the changing of millennia.

"I'll be 83 years old in November 1999," says Wilma Dean Dayton, who resides in a retirement community, "and I hope I die on my birthday. I don't want to see the world turn the corner into a whole new era, because I simply don't have the energy to deal with all that newness anymore."

"I remember my mother's talking about what it was like to be alive in 1900," says Marie Cisco, another retiree. "She was 42 or 43 at the time, I believe, and she lived to be 78. She had five children by then, and was to have one more when she was in her forties. She said she was too all-fired tired to take on a new century at the time, though she adjusted to it and even took an airplane ride before she died."

"Energy" is a key word in many millennial discussions. There is a general sense that turning the corner of a new millennium somehow releases a lot of psychological energy in the world. Young people, who are usually filled with energy anyway, greet this development with acceptance or excitement. But older persons often feel that their own energy is spent and that a resurgence of energy in the world around them will prove threatening or overwhelming.

"It makes me think of trying to hold the end of a fire hose when the water is turned on," says one man just reaching the age at which he can draw social security. "It can be a very frightening experience if you're not young enough and tough enough to hold that thing when it begins to buck and throw you!"

A woman who worked for a large corporation until she retired likens the coming of a new millennium to massive changes in the corporation. "When you're young and can stand changes, it's okay," she says. "But every wave of change knocks some of your feistiness and endurance out of you. Eventually you dread change, because you never know when you'll have reached your limit and it will simply carry you away."

Sadness and Depression

A lot of people, again predominantly among the elderly, face the prospects of a new millennium with melancholy spirits. If they have suffered a lot of pain and loss in the old century or if they feel depleted of energy, they regard the appearance of a whole new thousand years as an unwelcome, depressing event. They cannot conceive of themselves as thriving in a new era, and therefore prefer not to enter the era at all.

Juanita Waycroft, a psychologist in Minnesota, cautions that we should be very aware, in all the New Year's toasting and celebrations at the turn of the century, of the profound depression produced in some persons by such an event. "They may feel unable to cope with a new millennium," she says, "in the same way that an overworked clerk may feel completely overwhelmed by her boss's coming in and dumping a new load of responsibilities on her at the end of the day, when she is naturally tired and depleted. So instead of feeling elated and happy, they feel depressed and sad. Some may

even become suicidal, believing that life in a new age can hold absolutely nothing for them."

M. Bryan Nesbitt, an educational psychologist in Cambridge, Massachusetts, commented on a National Public Radio forum that some children as young as eight or ten, believing they have failed to please their parents or teachers, express suicidal thoughts, and that these thoughts often reach fulfillment in their teenage years, when pressure from peers, hormonal changes, and society in general simply becomes unbearable to them. This sense of depression and unworthiness, says Nesbitt, may well be augmented by the facing of a radically new era in the history of the world; the occasion that produces hope and excitement in the general public could work just the opposite effect on children who have poor self-images, and it is possible that we shall see an unprecedented wave of youth suicides as we approach the end of the century.

Certainly those who are lonely and dispirited by events in their lives in the old millennium will not feel overly optimistic about entering a new one, for they will see it as a grand extension of their present misery. Claire M. Butts, a widow for the past nine years, openly declares her preference not to enter a new millennium without her husband, Ralph. "We were close as two peas in a pod," she says, "and I still grieve every day about losing him. There just isn't the joy in things there used to be. You can imagine how I feel about crossing the threshold into a new era without him. It only aggravates the hurt. It's like I was being forced to take a long voyage and to leave all my reminders of him back at home. It isn't fair."

Terry Williams, a clerk in a convenience store, says, "Why should I look forward to a new age like that? I'm 46 years old. I lost two businesses in the last thirteen years. One was because my partner cheated me. He was siphoning off money out of our accounts and disappeared without a word to me about it. I lost everything—my business, my truck, my house, my family. My wife and kids left me because I didn't have anything left. The banks and lawyers picked me clean. I been working here two and a half years now. It doesn't pay much, but I'm eating. It doesn't matter to me that we're about to go into a new century, or even a new millennium. I won't even stay up to see the new year in."

If we look back through history for a comparable picture of the way world events can stimulate melancholy and depression, we are brought inevitably to the sixteenth and seventeenth centuries, when geographical expansion, the renaissance of learning, and challenges to old theological dicta produced a wave of melancholy that reverberated in most of the major writings of the era, from Sir Thomas Browne's *Hydriataphia, or Urn-Burial* to Shakespeare's gloomy *Hamlet* and Milton's *Paradise Lost*. Despair over the loss of tradition and stability in the world brought most sensible people to a feeling that life was moving faster than they wanted it to and that they couldn't cope with it any longer. Literary historians today often comment on the theme of decay and mutability running through so much of the public expression of the time.

It is easy to see how a similar theme winds its way through writings and films today. The last fifty years have been astonishing to practically everybody. Major technological innovations such as telecommunications, space travel, and the computer, coupled with incredible advances in medical research, changes in the popular lifestyle, and drastic alterations in many social institutions, including the church, have left many people feeling emotionally marooned, as if they were no longer in touch with their world, and unable to see how to bridge the gap. For a new century to open at such a time, and not just a new century but a new millennium, heaps an infinite sense of desperation on these persons, for the speed at which things change today promises unbeliev-

able transformations of human existence in the decades ahead. Sometimes even young writers and filmmakers betray a sense of nostalgia for a time when things didn't move so fast and life didn't keep catapulting so swiftly beyond our grasp.

In the sixties and seventies, the countercultural emphasis led to the Flower Children and the hippies. Today there is a corresponding movement among young professionals who opt to drop out of the race for more things and greater technology. They often retire to small towns or rural areas, simplify their existence, raise organic vegetables, spend a lot of time with their children, read and write books, practice meditative arts, and generally try to find life's meaning within themselves and their friends and families, not in the corporate structures of financial and productive America. These young (and sometimes middle-aged) people may not feel a sense of sadness about our entering a new millennium, but neither will they greet it with particular exuberance, for their distrust of trends in modern civilization will not encourage them to believe that time cures all ills or produces a finer society.

"A new millennium?" responds Clay Brokovski, a financial advisor who now works a few hours each day from his home in the country near Solvang, California. "It's only a construct. The earth, the plants and animals, won't notice. We'll get up on New Year's Day and face the same problems we had the year before, most of them springing from our indomitable greed and carelessness as human beings. And the promises of a galloping technology in the years ahead will only complicate things, because most people trust it as some kind of *deus ex machina* to rescue us from all our woes."

Anticipation and Excitement

For all the Terry Williamses and Clay Brokovskis, though, there are millions of people who become pumped up at the thought of living into a new millennium. For them it is almost as if the old millennium were a barrier restricting their existence, and when it is broken they will tumble out into a paradise of endless time and possibility. Actress Kathryn Walker, who began interviewing famous people in 1991 to ask whether they believe the year 2000 is a significant date, says that in the beginning the interviewees tended to look backwards at the old century and talk about such things as the Cold War and the collapse of the Soviet Union. But as we near the new millennium the tendency is in the other direction. People are becoming increasingly excited and hopeful.[5]

"I can hardly wait," says Bryce Sutherland of Mobile, Alabama. "I'm gonna be tooling around town in my '96 Camaro when it happens, and I'm gonna gun that thing up to 120 miles an hour and shout at the top of my lungs, 'cause it's gonna feel like I've broken the sound barrier or something and left my old life behind! Once we get there, I don't intend to look back. The sky's the limit in the new millennium!"

"I don't know," ponders Melanie Powers, a student at an eastern university, "it makes me feel all goose-pimply to be entering a new time zone like that. I know I probably won't be any different than I am right now, but I feel like maybe I will be or something. Maybe I'll be smarter or happier or whatever. It will be different from now. Life itself will be different."

"I'm 86 years old," says Benton R. Stephens, a retiree in Arizona. "I've lived through two world wars, the Great Depression, the Cold War, Korea, Vietnam, the Gulf War, the Oklahoma City bombing, and a helluva lot of other things. I'm looking forward to a clean slate, you know what I mean? A century in which there've been no killings, no rapes, no political or economic disasters, no crimes or mistakes of any kind. It will be nice just to start fresh. I think it will add ten years to my life."

"I'm not going to do anything special that New Year's Eve," says Brenda Goldwin, a hairstylist. "But I do intend to stay up and see the new year in. I think my heart will skip when I realize I've entered a whole new century that way. I may not even go to bed at all. My husband and I may just go out to the I-Hop for an early breakfast and then drive down to the beach and walk along it thinking about our future. I think it will be nice."

It is normal to feel a sense of exhilaration at new beginnings. Every new year produces at least a small feeling of excitement in most people, because it is a chance to start over, to renew friendships, rededicate oneself to a job or a relationship, deal with one's weaknesses and addictions, or simply hope for a better deal with the new deck of cards. Most of us make at least a couple of resolutions—to go on a diet, get up earlier, keep the house or office neater, clean out the basement, straighten the garage, take on fewer unnecessary assignments, spend more time with the children, go to church more regularly. There is hope and anticipation in getting the chance to start again, even if we have done it before and realize that our finest dreams and resolutions are soon dashed.

Psychologists say there is inevitably a kind of inner stimulus about reaching any goal or boundary—graduating from school, earning a new job status, or getting married. Crossing a line inspires new hopes and dreams, and becomes the reason for throwing ourselves more wholeheartedly into whatever we do, in the expectation that the future will be better than the past. Our adrenaline flows more rapidly when we begin a new year of school, take on a new challenge at work, join a new team, commit to a new organization, or make a new friend. Horizons beckon, our hearts beat faster, and our steps quicken.

"I can't retire until the year 2007," a pastor friend confided to me, "and frankly sometimes I don't know if I have the stamina to finish the course. But just thinking about a new millennium infuses me with the power to go on. It may not last, and by 2001 I may be singing the blues again. But somehow the thought of a span of time so new and pristine gives me the courage and strength to go ahead." He said the seven years left between the turn of the millennium and his eventual retirement reminded him of the significance of the number seven in Hebrew and Christian numerology. "It means fullness and completeness, you know. And somehow I expect them to be seven good years, not seven lean years."

Just as the amazing possibilities of new technology and an equal kind of human potential cause some people to feel overwhelmed and defeated when starting a new millennium, they stimulate unbounded hope and energy in others. "We are only in the foothills of computer technology," stated Wayne G. Bishop at a meeting of computer specialists in Hampton Roads, Virginia. "By the year 2010 we'll be getting into the mountains. By 2025 we'll be in the heights. Then we may just take off for the sky!"

Peter C. Newman, writing in *Maclean's* about the effect of the new millennium on Canadians, predicts that people in his country will find things very different then. There will be a new stress on the quality of life, he thinks, as opposed to the standard of living. People will rely more on character than on personality, which has become so important in this century. "Nothing will feel the same, because the millennium will have placed borders around our experience, no less real than the borders on a map."[6]

For those with the interest and energy to care about the future of life on the planet, the opening years of a new millennium are filled with special promise. Biologists are excited about all that will be learned about DNA, cloning, and other facets of their science. Cancer and AIDS specialists expect to see cures for these diseases developed shortly into the new millennium. The technology is already here for

great advances in the way we employ computers, so that every home and office will be revolutionized in the coming decades. New chemical compounds and metals promise to enhance our existence in areas most of us don't even think about now. Energy specialists promise radically innovative vehicles for travel and ways of heating and cooling our homes and businesses. Educationists are just beginning to wrestle creatively and productively with the possibilities of computer learning for home schooling at every level from preschool to graduate training. Even the way we handle our shopping, barter, and exchange will change dramatically, with so-called "smart cards" replacing money, checks, and conventional banking.

The twenty-first century should find us all in better health and nutrition, with more time for sports and relaxation, with safer and more reliable modes of transportation, and with greater cultural resources for understanding ourselves and our relationships than we have ever enjoyed before. We should live longer, learn faster, experience less pain, enjoy more effortless travel, have more fun, and feel more prosperous. Those concerned with the ecosystem should see encouraging data about pollution, the ozone layer, and the regenerative power of the earth. Readers should have more books to choose from, moviegoers more movies, coffee-lovers more kinds of coffee, and travelers more exotic places to go. In short, the situations in which we exist should continue to improve, provided that our attitudes are positive and we can adapt to changes without longing for the way things were or short-circuiting a better environment through excessive greed and selfishness.

As Jerry Adler writes in *Newsweek*,

> If you had fun in the 20th century, or even if you didn't, you will find it almost impossible to avoid in the 21st. Working ever harder to keep your place in the world economy, you will

seek out fun in compensatory doses. Fun in the next century will be of much higher quality, because there will be so many more playoff games in comparison to the regular season, a trend clearly in evidence in last year's baseball schedule. And outdoor fun will be better than ever. There won't be any new mountains, but the ones already in place will be exploited even more imaginatively by people climbing up them, and sliding, rolling, rappelling or hang-gliding down. Try to escape fun and it will seek you out anyway, at your hotel or restaurant, where eating will increasingly be impossible without the accompaniment of 32 bedsheet-size TV screens showing highlights from the World Cup quarterfinals.[7]

Why shouldn't we feel expansive and excited as the new millennium approaches? When we think of the light-years of progress and enlightenment that have occurred since the last millennial shift, in the year 1000 C.E., we have every reason to be encouraged. Then, physicians treated patients with leeches, bleeding, and alchemy, and the mentally imbalanced were put to death or consigned to dungeons. Transportation was limited to ships and animals, and even the great Roman roads, once the life-arteries of Europe, had fallen into ruin and disrepair. Communication was effected by couriers, smoke signals, and drums, and by the time people learned that a king or pope had done some infamous deed, he was already replaced by another. Schooling existed primarily for the royal or the wealthy, who were usually the same persons, and books were inscribed by hand, one letter and one page at a time. People who were a little strange were usually accused of witchcraft, which meant their lives as well as their properties were forfeit to the accusers. Everything that happened was believed to be the action of either a god or a devil, and even the science of Aristotle and the ancient Egyptians, respectable for their times, had given way to the most abysmal ignorance and superstition.

Is it any wonder that some people dream eagerly of the progress of another millennium? What will the world be like on the eve of the year 3000 C.E.? Will all illnesses have been eradicated, and all mental disorders as well? Will there be a single world government, and general enlightenment around the globe, so that no one suffers because of race, creed, or disability? With or without nuclear families, will there be a general sense of welfare among all people, with great care given universally to the rearing of children and the enjoyment of life? Will there be spiritual unanimity and a widespread sense of balance between the spiritual and physical realms? Will technology serve everyone without abusing, disenfranchising, or penalizing any? Will the world seem to be the best of all possible worlds and will there be anything else to hope for in the arrival of a fourth millennium after Christ?

Hope and expectancy are good for us, we are told; they engender health in the body and a beneficial interaction between the mind and the physical being. People who are hopeful and expectant recover more quickly from normal illnesses and are less likely to succumb to cancer and other life-threatening diseases. They interact more pleasantly with friends and colleagues. They live longer and are more productive. So why shouldn't the approach of a new millennium be greeted with excitement and enthusiasm? Why shouldn't its promise make us more lighthearted and hopeful? It would be foolish to become giddy and unduly optimistic about the changing of millennia, of course; Clay Brokovski was right, the earth will not notice, the plants and animals will go on as usual, millennia are only mental constructs. But perhaps anything that lifts our hearts and promises newness and progress is worth focusing on for the next few months. The results of our expectancy alone may prove helpful and beneficial to us all.

The Importance of Hope

It is impossible to overestimate the importance of hope in the human heart. It has been known to save romances, start important organizations, build cities, and even keep people alive.

And hope has often been related to time.

"Time cures all," we have said from time immemorial.

"Time will tell," we say.

Given enough time, we expect inequities to be righted, wounds to be healed, grievances to be forgiven and forgotten, and love to prevail. Time doesn't save everything, of course. Time also produces weathering, erosion, loss, and death. But we expect those things. They are part of the natural order and the way things work. It is also natural to believe that some things will improve with time, that there is an anabasis as well as a katabasis in human affairs, a going up as well as a falling down.

"Hope springs eternal in the human heart." It is a true saying, even though hope may not spring very high or far if it has been trodden under foot long enough or hard enough. And there is probably nothing in human existence more important than hope, than the belief that somehow things will improve, life will get better, and there will be a happy ending to everything.

How many times have we heard people in sorrow or difficulty quote the words of Paul in Romans, "We know that all things work together for good for those who love God, who are called according to his purpose" (Romans 8:28)? It is a rather preposterous saying, on the face of it. *All* things? Even vast disappointments and gross inequities? Even enormous reverses and irreparable losses? Yet there is something in the promise that keeps us going in the worst of times, that nourishes that little flicker of hope that continues to burn down under the rubble of bad experiences and constant disasters.

Victor Frankl once said that more people died in concen-

tration camps from a loss of hope than from disease, malnutrition, and extermination. People must have hope to survive. It is the one thing that must be left to them when all else fails, or there is no will to live at all.

What is our calling as preachers but to engender hope? In the dark of the night, when the fever rages and the storm howls, that is our commission, our assignment, our justification: we are the sweet singers of hope. We whisper the rumor of faith into the ears of those who have surrendered children to drugs and high-speed automobile crashes, those who have lost jobs and reputations and incomes, those who have been deserted by parents or spouses or children, those whose bodies are wracked by pain and whose hearts are wrecked by despair, those who are traveling inexorably toward death and the far horizon. And at the end of a millennium, when appetites are jaded by too much of everything but love and presence and community, when many are afraid of the future lest it be worse than the past that has disappointed and mauled them, when it is all but impossible to believe that life can be sweeter and better and more meaningful than it has been, it is our task, our responsibility, our *privilege* to speak words of comfort and expectation, words of sober hope and deep joy, about life and where it is going and what God intends for it in the years ahead.

How we shall do it is at least partly clothed in mystery, for thank God mystery is part of our calling too, is so entangled with it that the two shall never be extricated from each other. And even after it is done it shall remain at least partly mysterious, for there is no analysis sufficient to explain a mystery, any more than we can fathom the inner meaning of sea shells or cyclones or lichen or dust. But it has something to do with intent and faithfulness, with knowing we are bearers of the hopeful word and continuing to preach that word year in and year out until we are hoarse in the throat and daft in the mind.

James Carse, in that marvelous book *Breakfast at the Victory*, tried to talk about the mystery of great teaching and how it occurs. In the end he had to point to Socrates, one of the greatest of all teachers, and ask what made him so powerful an instructor. Socrates didn't really teach anything, Carse concludes; there was no body of material he was attempting to impart. Instead he questioned those who did teach or aver. He probed and twisted and argued and distorted, and in the end his students emerged as wiser and better persons, chastened by their encounter with the whirlwind, their submergence in the deep currents of their teacher's mind. And each went away, says Carse, with new thoughts and understandings in his head. The greatness of Socrates lay not in the manner in which he conveyed information to others but in the way people thought new thoughts and dreamed new dreams while engaged in conversation with him.

Isn't that the way it is with great preaching as well? It isn't anything we have to say, any great schema we have to impart, that really speaks to people's hearts. It is the way we weave the spells that will enchant them into thinking about things for themselves, the way we tempt them into rehearsing matters they wouldn't ordinarily rehearse.

There was an elderly woman in my parish in Los Angeles, a schoolteacher named Margaret Noe, who told me what it was like for her to go to church when James Fifield was the minister. "I loved to hear him speak," she said, "for he always opened new vistas in my mind and I would be entranced by the thoughts I experienced. Afterwards I never went through the line to shake hands with him, but always went directly outside to the fountain in the courtyard, where I could sit alone for half an hour still pursuing the thoughts that had been started in the sermon."

New vistas in the mind are what we ought to offer every time we preach. And the approach of the millennium should

provide an almost unparalleled occasion for tapping those new vistas, for conjuring visions of life and relationship and meaning even beyond those of which our people are ordinarily capable. Military chaplains say that they rarely experience a situation so ripe for preaching as when troops are first going overseas, especially if they are being sent to a battle zone; the very newness and strangeness of the men and women's future, the fact that they are on the eve of life-altering encounters, renders them peculiarly susceptible to the moods and ideas of the sermon. Shouldn't the same be true for people entering a new millennium in which no one has yet drawn breath or spoken a word? What a sacred landscape the new millennium is, how fraught with holy possibilities!

Even the congregants who are as jaded as Didi and Gogo in Beckett's *Waiting for Godot*, so that they aren't sure whether Godot is coming or not, or if they will recognize him when he does, must feel a glimmer of hope somewhere deep in their psyches, as if the new era will bring them unexpected opportunities, untried experiences, and unimagined journeys. Even those who had renounced hope altogether will surely set aside their renunciations for a little while, and admit the possibility that something new and friendly might occur to them, that they might be surprised by a sense of trust and expectancy in the unfolding of a brand-new segment of time.

I may be wrong, but it seems to me that the amazing surge of spirituality (or at least the hunger for it) in the last couple of decades has something to do with our disappointments in the old millennium and our unconscious feeling of hope as a new one approaches. It has really occurred against all odds. Americans have never been better off, if we gauge welfare by employment, material success, housing starts, automobile and TV and computer sales, the growth of suburbs and malls, travel opportunities, and general health. Yet somehow, in an age that has witnessed the end of the Cold War, increased welfare and retirement benefits, and the relative guarantee of security to citizens of our country, we have known a strange and gnawing hunger for something more, something that neither the welfare state nor military security nor abundance of food and entertainment could supply: we have wanted to recover our rootedness in God, and to unearth in a world of shifting values a sense of ultimate meaning. We have looked at our plethora of Wal-Marts and Circuit Cities and Pizza Huts and Food Kings and cable companies and have remembered the haunting line of Peggy Lee's famous song, "Is that all there is?" And we have said no, there is more, much more, but it doesn't lie on the surface of things and it can't be bought with a charge card or found in a supermall. It has to do with such invisible, intangible things as presence, spirit, soul, and love, and can be found only through the depths of the heart and the intent of the will.

We all secretly hope, I believe, that the new millennium will turn out to be a time of release and renewal, when we not only rediscover God but rediscover God with such a sense of immediacy and power that it will make even the ages of faith in the sixteenth and seventeenth centuries look like a mere nursery-school attempt at capturing spirituality. And if the preacher is asleep at the switch and does not take advantage of this deep, underlying desire for newness and God, it will be tragic for the people in his or her care, and for the preacher as well. All of them together will have missed out on one of the rare bonus eras in the history of humanity, when the flow of what Jung called the great collective unconscious and the flow of the preacher's rhetoric might well have joined together to form a flood tide of faith and expectancy!

Great Biblical Themes That Find Resonance in the Approach of a New Millennium

In the last chapter I mentioned the famous psychiatrist Carl Jung's idea of the collective unconscious, that there are archetypes of idea and experience that persist in the human mind with uncanny universality, as though they were transmitted from generation to generation by DNA or some other as yet undiscovered miracle of regeneration. Jung and his followers have amply demonstrated how the great myths of ancient times repeatedly play themselves out in human consciousness and how our dreams are often structured around such classical themes and stories even though in our waking moments we are totally unaware of their existence. We don't have to be Jungians to understand that the greatest motifs or constructs of the human mind are those that find amplification again and again throughout history, recurring with incredible regularity in the poetry, art, drama, and folklore of every nation on earth, irrespective of tongue or education.

The Bible has contributed mightily to the store of images

and ideas that get repeated in this manner. The pictures of Adam and Eve being turned out of Paradise, Cain slaying his brother Abel, Abraham preparing to sacrifice his son Isaac, Moses leading the Israelites through the wilderness, Joseph rising to power over his family, David slaying Goliath, Mary giving birth to a special Child, Judas betraying Jesus, the early Christians speaking in other tongues at the festival of Pentecost have all become part of a set of universal constructs for pondering and understanding human existence, and as such appear even in the art and poetry of people whose heritage is not related directly to that of Jews and Christians. We actually find ourselves reliving these stories and pictures, or at least analyzing portions of our lives on the basis of them, for they help us to think about life and meaning in ways we could not grasp without them.

Edward P. Wimberly, in *Prayer in Pastoral Counseling*, describes his practice of using these recurrent images as structures around which counselees can describe and understand their life experiences. One patient, for example, was having difficulty facing the hardships of her life because she always believed they would overcome her. Wimberly asked her to name an attitude in the Bible that reflected her own. She chose the one of the spies who returned to Joshua and announced that the Israelites could not move into the promised land because it was filled with giants. Wimberly told her to read the section about the eventual capture of Jericho and the entry into the promised land, and to consider how she could make that an image for her future living. Soon she became more triumphal about her life and was able to deal with her problems in an increasingly confident attitude, for she was anchored not in a story about defeatism but in one about success and overcoming.

Literary critics usually agree that one of the dimensions which great works of literature have in common is that they manage somehow to touch the strata of story and symbol that

lie buried deeply beneath them, in the accumulating stories and symbols of the ages. Thus Ernest Hemingway's greatest achievement among all his notable writings was undoubtedly *The Old Man and the Sea*, in which the old fisherman Santiago draws on the power of stories and myths before him, such as the Fisher King and Odysseus, and the large fish Santiago catches is somehow related to Moby Dick, Jonah's great fish, and other significant fish stories of the ages. Readers may not realize that they are more deeply impressed by Santiago's story because of its resonance with other classical tales, but they are. *The Sun Also Rises, A Farewell to Arms*, and *For Whom the Bell Tolls* are great novels too. But in none of them does Hemingway so powerfully border on the mythological as he does in *The Old Man and the Sea*, and it is this transparency to other great stories of history that lends the last novel its classical depth and poignancy.

Correspondingly, one of the tricks thoughtful preachers learn about their craft is that certain sermons derive enormous power from the potency of the original images reincarnated in them. Take the story of the prodigal son, for example, which has proved so mighty a tool in the hands of talented evangelists. How deftly it describes the rebelliousness of the young against their parents and traditions, and then the painfulness of discovering that the parents were not so blind and stupid after all, and that the world is an exceedingly hard place in which to live alone, without the support of friends and family. Who among us has not at some time been caught by such a story and made to remember feelings directed at our own parents? Who has not suffered the humiliation of defeat and the torture of loneliness, and wished to have things back the way they used to be? Who has not wanted to sit again at father's or mother's table and be part of a family that has since drifted or fallen apart? The sermon based on the story of the prodigal son thus begins with a hidden power to succeed and compel, for it draws on the mythological structures that lie beneath the human story itself.

This is why, in considering how to deal in sermons with the approach of the new millennium, it is wise to begin with the great paradigms in scripture, to see how they lend themselves as motifs and patterns for facing a new time. Think, for instance, of the very first construct in the Bible, the story of Creation in Genesis.

Creation and Creativity

Genesis. "In the beginning." Imagine the newness, the freshness!

Think about attending the theater or the opera. There are discordant sounds at first from the orchestra pit as the various musicians tune their instruments. Then there are discernible arrangements to some of the notes. Finally the entire orchestra begins to play together, the curtains part, and a new world is born on the stage.

Could this be a picture of the way the world began? Nothing at first. Darkness and void. Then something starting. A noise, a flash, something coming into existence. Again. The world is beginning to be. And then it is there, the trees still dripping from the bringing together of desert and sea, field and river, and debris lying about before the Creator has had a chance to sweep up. Lights up! Full orchestra! Curtains back! Behold the earth!

The creativity motif runs throughout the scriptures:

First, the world, the sun, and the moon. The animals and birds and creatures of the sea.

Then man and woman, and the family.

Then the Sabbath.

Then ethics—rules for behavior.

Noah makes an ark, according to specifications provided by God.

God makes the rainbow.

God makes a covenant with Abraham. Abraham, in turn, makes a covenant with Abimelech. Abraham's grandson Jacob makes a covenant with Laban.

Making becomes a way of life. People make alliances, altars, arks, tabernacles, and songs. Eventually cities and temples and celebrations.

Jeremiah, who is as sensitive to history as he is to the future, describes God as a potter who is fashioning a vessel on the wheel. Israel, he says, is a spoiled pot. Does it want to be removed from the wheel and dashed on the ground? If not, it had better shape up for Yahweh, become more flexible and malleable in the divine hands, give up its idolatrous ways.

God is still in a making mood, says Jeremiah, and will create a new covenant, one etched in the hearts of the people.

More than that, says Jesus, God is making a new Israel, a kingdom of derelicts, a congregation of true believers and followers. This calls for new signs—a prophet baptizing in Jordan, a teacher on the mountain (in Matthew) and in the valleys (in Luke), a man with healing in his touch and forgiveness in his heart, death on a cross, the Resurrection, a Pentecostal gathering, earthen vessels bearing a great treasure, visions of eschatological wonder, a new city not made with hands.

It is no wonder that all this making has become the fount for the greatest outpouring of art and drama and music and devotion and fiction and scholarship in the history of the world. Making generates making. Art begets art. Life keeps reconstituting itself.

What a natural theme it all is for the turning of the millennia, for the releasing of creative powers as humankind lurches forward into unplowed fields of time, fresh and eager to make the first marks on an unspoiled landscape! How easily people can identify with the sense of freshness at the beginning of time, with the chance to devise better worlds, create more equity among nations, establish governments that bless and comfort, build relationships of truth and caring, nourish communities capable of redemption, support, and love. "In the beginning." The very words ring with hope and encouragement, for we too shall have a beginning, a chance to start again and become what we've always wished we could be.

Sermon titles leap to mind: "Makers with God," "The Hovering Spirit," "Becoming Fruitful in a New Time," "Receiving the Breath of Life Again," "Sensitive to the Potter's Touch," "Building and Blessing," "From Creation to Recreation," "Made in the Image (or Images) of God," "Looking for a City."

The preacher could even preach a series of sermons on creation, while the church could celebrate creativity with an arts festival, featuring exhibits of members' handiwork, special musical programs, important films, readings, book reviews, and discussions of the way God is still at work in the world through the visions of various kinds of makers, including artists, architects, chefs, city planners, decorators, landscapers, musicians, and writers.

Journey

One of the dominant themes of the Christian faith, according to the writer of Hebrews, is that of the journey into uncharted territories. It began with Abraham, who left Ur of the Chaldees, one of the most amazing cities of ancient times, and led his family and servants out on a wilderness pilgrimage that lasted for years, all because God told him to go. It was revived in spades by the wilderness wanderings of the Israelites under Moses and Joshua, an episode in Jewish history that would leave its imprint on the national consciousness forever. Jesus was born while his parents were on a journey, and was soon after taken into Egypt, as if somehow to reverse the direction of the Israelites when they sought the promised land. His whole ministry appears to have involved constant travel, and in the Fourth Gospel he is represented as declaring, "I am the Way, the Truth, and the Life," the Way indicating that one comes to Truth and Life not by static commitment but by journeying toward them. Paul's journeys became epic events in the life of the early church, Odyssean in character but reaching beyond Odysseus in terms of what they bequeathed to the world.

All of these, and countless others, says the author of Hebrews, "wandered in deserts and mountains, and in caves and holes in the ground" (Hebrews 11:38). Yet they didn't receive all that God had to give them because they could not be made perfect without us. "Therefore," intones that great, ringing peroration at the beginning of Hebrews 12, "since we are surrounded by so great a cloud of witnesses, let us also lay aside every weight and the sin that clings so closely, and let us run with perseverance the race that is set before us, looking to Jesus the pioneer and perfecter of our faith, who for the sake of the joy that was set before him endured the cross, disregarding its shame, and has taken his seat at the right hand of the throne of God" (Hebrews 12:1-2).

The opening of a new millennium is a time for faith and for journeys. The beckoning new horizons suddenly extend far beyond the old ones. The new era becomes a time for girding ourselves and making commitments for pilgrimage.

It is surely no wonder that John Bunyan, the great seventeenth-century dissenter, cast his epic story of a man's struggle to follow Christ in the form of a journey and called him Pilgrim. Or that Kurt Vonnegut in his modern novel *Slaughterhouse Five* called his modest hero Billy Pilgrim, probably in recollection of Bunyan's protagonist. Life is a journey, and all of us are travelers. And a time like this, when one millennium is sloughed off and another begun, is a time for contemplating journeys and where they lead.

Again the sermon titles are legion: "Journey into Tomorrow," "New Opportunities and Deeper Commitments," "On the Road to God's Future," "All the Way Home," "Mileposts to God," "The Path to the Self That Lies Through God," "Wayfarers in a Strange Land," "The End of One Road and the Beginning of Another," "Where Paths Converge," "The Way to the City of God," "Beggars by the Roadway of Life," "The Trip to Forever," and "Highway to Heaven."

Jubilee

There is little evidence that the biblical idea of Jubilee was ever practiced, but its roots lie deep in the mingled mercy and discipline of God's people. Theoretically it was the fiftieth year following every cycle of seven seven-year or sabbatical periods in Israel's history. It was a special time when the fields were to lie fallow, all land was returned to its original owners, and Israelite slaves were freed from bondage. As described in Leviticus 25 and 27 and Numbers 36, it was supposed to begin with the blowing of the shofar on the Day of Atonement (the Hebrew *yovel*, from which the name Jubilee is derived, was the word for the ram's horn used as a shofar) and end a year later, when a new cycle of seven-year periods began.

The notion of Jubilee, apart from its actual practice, has always been an important one, and has surfaced from time to time in Christian history as a symbol of the generosity with which we are to regard the earth, the holding of property, the use of animals, and the dignity of other human beings. Martin Luther King, Jr., for example, was fond of the term and often cited it as a call to Christian followers in our day.

Because Jubilee was essentially a concept regarding time and time-cycles, it is an extremely appropriate theme to sound as this millennium draws to a close and another is about to commence. Its proclamation can underline the fact that time needs to be sanctified by prayer and recommitment to God, and it can easily become a call to higher living as we approach a new era. Dom Gregory Dix wrote a classic scholarly book a few years ago called *The Shape of the Liturgy* in which he demonstrated that the canonical hours of monastic and clerical life are in reality an attempt to sanctify all time and ought therefore to be viewed as one of the most essential constructs of human existence. In the same way it is easy to view the transition from one century to another and one millennium to another as very important moments in the ongoing life of the race, and therefore of critical significance for reassessment of purpose and rededication of selves and gifts.

In England, the Christian Aid society is circulating a "Jubilee 2000 Petition," seeking twenty-two million signatures worldwide to call on the leaders of wealthy nations to forgive the debts of the world's poorest countries. "We, the undersigned," reads the petition, "believe that the start of the new millennium should be a time to give hope to the impoverished people of the world. To make a fresh start, we believe it right to put behind us the mistakes made by both lenders and borrowers and to cancel the backlog of unpayable debts of the most impoverished nations."

Sermons on the Jubilee theme might emphasize the importance of our pausing at this vital juncture to reconsider what God intended for the earth and humanity and reflect on what we can do in the coming years to restore both the earth and ourselves to divine care. They could stress the ecological note in the original proclamation of Jubilee (letting the fields lie fallow) and challenge the congregation to daily concern for the fate of our globe. They could raise questions about the greed and avarice that mark our attitudes toward property and remind us that the earth is the Lord's, not ours, and that we are to live as servants, not masters. And they could emphasize the importance of forgiveness and restitution for those who have wronged us, as well as equality for those who are treated as virtual slaves in our society. They might even raise questions about penal codes and prison reform that are too seldom addressed by Christian communities, even though the New Testament frequently stresses our relationship to prisoners.

Titles for such sermons might include: "The Jubilation of Our Times," "A Time of Cleansing and Forgiveness," "Restoring the Earth to Its Rightful Owner," "Sanctifying the New Millennium," "Remembering Who We Are at the Turn of the Millennium," "Dying with Christ to Live for the Future," and "Letting All the Slaves Go Free."

Returning to the Tabernacle

The tabernacle (Hebrew *mishkan*) was a large portable sanctuary described in Exodus 25–30 which was supervised by the Levites and served the Israelites as a sort of pre-temple (some scholars believe the description of an extremely large tent, some 72 feet by 145 feet, was an exaggerated description based on later knowledge of the temple itself). Consisting of great curtains supported on poles, it supposedly contained a Holy of Holies with the ark of the covenant, the altar of incense, the seven-branched lampstand, and a table for the bread of the Presence. Theoretically it was moved wherever the Israelites went in their wilderness wanderings and stood in the center of their camp, with the Levites encamped nearest to it and the other tribes arranged systematically around it.

Regardless of how factual or unfactual the descriptions may have been, the tabernacle has always had enormous significance for the Jewish faith, for it symbolizes a place of meeting with God that can be moved with the people wherever they go, as opposed to the temple, which for all its splendor remained stationary in Jerusalem. A temple is fine

in an era of peace and stability when people can come and go to Jerusalem as they please. But in times of turmoil and chaos—of which Israel had plenty—the tabernacle remained a valuable reminder of God's loving-kindness and fidelity which never left them alone.

The preaching of tabernacle faith can be very significant as we are about to embark on an entirely new millennium when traditional institutions are under threat and the future is uncertain. Most Christians are aware today of the serious erosion of denominational structures and a general departure from the cultural prominence enjoyed by the Christian religion in earlier generations. As Peter Berger and Thomas Luckmann pointed out in *The Social Construction of Reality*, most people's understandings of God and religious philosophy are determined by what the society holds as true and important, not by an individual commitment to the search for truth. It is not as easy to hold an unqualified belief in the existence of God today, and a sure understanding of what it means to serve God, as it was in a time when the religious communities were unified and in control of our culture. Whereas American Christians once seldom encountered religious beliefs and practices very different from their own, now they pass Muslim mosques and Buddhist temples on their way to work or school, hear the declarations of secularism and agnosticism broadcast daily on radio and TV, and generally live among the nonreligious assumptions of modern science and technology. Some have reacted to this by attempting to draw their congregations into tight-knit circles that insist on the inerrant truth of their traditions and beliefs over against the free circulation of counterclaims in the society. Some have tried to find ways of compromising and blending tradition and other viewpoints. But it is obviously a time of testing for Christian communities, and the testing is likely to grow more severe as we cross the line into a new millennium.

For this reason it is easy to imagine ourselves as living in a time of new wilderness, when the way to the future remains largely uncharted and the promised land has become more elusive than ever. This means that the concept of tabernacle, of God's traveling with us on an uncertain way, has assumed a new importance in our age. Our temples of denominational experience and theological certainty are crumbling. We find ourselves once again on the Way, trying to make sense of new experiences and to discern what it means to serve God in such an unpredictable environment.

The tabernacle is not a symbol inferior to that of the temple. On the contrary, the pressures and trials we are now experiencing make it more vital, more important, more crucial to us. It suggests that God is still moving, as we are, and still observing a covenant whose roots are millennia old. God is still being faithful to promises made in the earliest times of history.

Some people, of course, have become addicted to their temples. They find it hard to leave behind their idolatries, their shibboleths, their sanctified traditions. They spend their time and energy complaining about the loss of cherished ideals and understandings, about the way God appears to have abandoned them and the formulas for religious life that served them so long and so well. But that is part of the preacher's challenge, to persuade them that Jesus himself (especially in the Gospel of Mark) was anti-temple and predicted the end of an age of templelike security, and that if we seriously intend to follow Jesus into the next millennium we shall learn to "go to him outside the camp" (Hebrews 13:13), seeking a city and tradition not made by human hands. The tabernacle has always been a more fit symbol of Christianity than the temple, but never more so than at the beginning and in our own era. As the late Daniel T. Niles of Sri Lanka liked to say, "There ought to be a placard saying 'Move On' over the head of every Christian."

Sermon titles? How about: "The Christ Who Goes Before Us," "Moving into a New Millennium with God," "Passport to Eternity," "Trusting in God, Not Institutions," "What Can You Believe in a Time When It's Hard to Believe Anything?" "Carrying the Church into the New Millennium," "Living with a Presence That Keeps Moving On," and "People Who Live in Tents Don't Get Hit by Falling Stones."

The Cross, the Resurrection, and New Life

When we think about it we realize that Christianity was actually born in a time of cultural chaos not unlike our own. Palestine was occupied by the Romans with their pantheon of gods and goddesses and their continuing attempt to syncretize all religions in order to miss nothing. Tarsus, the city in the province of Cilicia where the apostle Paul grew up, was a microcosm of religious traditions and understandings, for it was home to Jews, Asiatics, Syrians, Persians, and Phoenicians as well as Greeks and Romans, and prided itself on its openness to all traditions. The fertility cults flourished there alongside ancient philosophies, and Apollonius, a noted philosopher trained in the city, withdrew to a more remote area because he said a miasma of perversion and immorality hung over the place. Among the Jews themselves, religious practice had degenerated into the nitpicking legalism of the scribes and Pharisees, and many of the common people generally ignored the spiritual life altogether.

The hope that focused on Christ drew upon ancient traditions of a vital faith and practice in Israel while at the same time recognizing something excitingly new and unpredicted in his mien and understanding. He did not come as a golden warrior or untouchable high priest but as a humble man, a servant unafraid to touch the sores of the leper or to dine in the homes of the unwashed. His kingdom, while expected to rejuvenate the earthly dominion of Israel, had something definitely unearthly about it. It laid more emphasis on prayer and presence than it did on princely power and might. In the end, Christ himself did not shrink from the death of a common criminal, and submitted to it with a glory and equanimity that impressed even his executioners. And when the Resurrection came, with its scenes of comic fear and misunderstanding as well as its portrait of regal transcendence, it confirmed a formula that God had apparently intended all along: the way to life is through dying, the route to heavenly coronation lies through willing humiliation. The Cornerstone that the builders had rejected because it looked too weak and bereft of earthly power God had made to become the foundation of everything, the bulwark of an eternal reign.

Thus Resurrection and New Life became the theme and symbol of the early church, itself composed of the broken, the weak, the humble of the world. Those despised by empire and tradition became endowed with the power to rewrite history and change the world. The blood of the martyrs became the seed of a glorious new Way, one that would exist for millennia as a vital, pulsating force in human affairs, leading the poet W. B. Yeats, nearly two thousand years later, to write in "The Second Coming" of the world as a "rough beast" that "slouches towards Bethlehem to be born."

As preachers we would be remiss if we did not at the end of one age and the beginning of another proclaim regularly the power of the Crucified and Raised-Up Christ, as much an enigma to our age as it was to that of the early Christians, yet still the heart and core of the faith we claim to have. Is the new millennium threatening to old ways and habits? Do we fear the newness, the unknown? The securest stance is that of Jesus himself, who though he enjoyed being with God poured out his self-interest and became as we are, in order that God might raise us all to newness of life in him. The

Cross and the Resurrection are still the key to meaning and triumph for every believer.

Sermon titles? "Jesus Christ, the Same Yesterday, Today, and Forever," "The Primacy of the Cross in the Life of the Christian," "A New Era for the Lord of All New Eras," "Lord of the Waves," "Fundamentals of the Faith in an Age of Inconsequentials," "The Hope of the World and the Gift of Tomorrow," "Dying for Christ in the New Millennium," "The Unrivaled Power of the Great Christian Ideas," "The Kingdom That Shall Not Be Shaken."

Fellowship and Community

The *koinonia* or fellowship band in the early church was all-important to the survival of individual Christians and of the church as well. In an age of conflicting beliefs and ideologies when people could be punished for their faith in Christ, members of the body of Christ needed one another for support and encouragement; otherwise they were prone to defect from the church and return to beliefs and practices more acceptable to the Roman Empire. Fully 80 percent of the New Testament material appears to have been written with at least one eye on the temptations people felt to desert the faith. When congregants prayed the model prayer of Jesus with its words "Bring us not to the test," they knew full well that the test was not some trivial temptation such as greed or immorality but the most awful test of all, to forsake the faith once chosen. This is one reason the apostle Paul felt it so incumbent on him wherever he went to establish fellowship groups for new Christians. It was not enough merely to see them converted and living individually for Christ. Paul knew that without the active urging and support of others they would all die like embers lying apart from the fire.

The same is surely true today. We live in an age when there are more people crowded into most spaces than ever before. Yet there is also today an enormous sense of isolation and loneliness among people. Even those who work in crowded offices and walk the busy streets of our metropolises and drive in rush-hour traffic confess to feeling alone, without anyone except perhaps one or two family members and an odd friend or two who really knows or cares who they are. Most of the funniest sitcoms on television—*Seinfeld, Frasier, Cybil, Murphy Brown, Drew Carey*—are about people who are unbearably fragile and lonely even though they spend their time with other people suffering from the same problems.

The Christian pulpit still has a message of hope for these people. It is about a Christ who showed us the fullness of love and sharing by laying down his life for us, and who commands us to love one another as he loved us. Of course it is an age of cynicism and relativism, and we can't simply talk about love, we have to demonstrate it, actually involve people in it. But where else in the world can people turn to find such a foundation for fellowship and hope? The civic clubs? The government? Voluntary organizations? To the extent that any of them offer fellowship and community at all, they derived them from Christianity, whose ways and ideas have permeated Western thought. But the possibility of real community, with love and loyalty and total commitment, remains highest in the church, which is the mother of such qualities throughout the world.

"There are many reasons to give up on the church today," says a minister friend of mine, "and I think I've rehearsed them a hundred times or more. But as long as a lonely boy or girl finds fellowship in a Sunday school teacher or group leader who cares about them, as long as a pitiful-looking young woman can come to prayer meeting and sit there with a glow on her face because it's the one place in the town where she thinks someone cares that she's there, as long as an old couple who've recently moved to the neighborhood can come and hold hands through a service and be greeted warmly by other people afterwards, I'm not going to give up. For all its faults, the church is still the number-one place for love and fellowship in the world, even ahead of the family, which is often dysfunctional and disheartening. No, I'll hold on to the church as long as I myself can still go there and sit on a pew and feel that Christ is there, welcoming me to that great host of witnesses and whispering in my ear, 'Go find someone else and tell him that you love him.' I'll hold on because I don't know of another organization in the world where this is regarded as being of such supreme importance. I won't give up on the church as long as there is the least bit of love in it."

The Bible is filled with great precedents, all the way from the book of Genesis and the Garden of Eden to the book of Revelation and the picture of the heavenly city, for preaching love and faithfulness and commitment to one another. And of course nowhere does the theme reach loftier heights than in the practice and teaching of Christ and his sacrificial death on the cross.

The twenty-first century may be an age of technology and space travel and unnerving change, but it need not be a time of consuming individuality, distrust, and loneliness. Our preaching has but to rise to meet the challenge of the times, offering people the possibilities of love, support, and fellowship.

Sermon titles for this might include: "Finding Christ's Presence Through Your Neighbor," "Putting People First in the Twenty-First," "Discovering the Power of Three or Four," "Living Heart-to-Heart Instead of Hand-to-Mouth," "The Fellowship Where Differences Dissolve," "What If Christians Discovered How to Love?" "Following Christ from the Garden of Betrayal to the Cross of Forgiveness," and "Finding Love in the Midst of a Crowd."

Sacrifice and Service

Robert Bellah and his sociologist colleagues who wrote *Habits of the Heart* and *The Good Society*, among the most formidable analyses of American society in the last two decades, agreed on one thing: America has become such an individualistic nation that the whole concept of the voluntary organization is greatly endangered. When Alexis de Toqueville wrote *Democracy in America* more than a hundred and sixty years ago, he saw the voluntary association as one of the striking hallmarks of our country. There were thousands of such associations, he declared, filled with people eager to make a difference in their surroundings. Today, say Bellah and his coauthors, the percentage of Americans willing to sacrifice their time and energy for the good of the whole is quite small. In fact, they say:

> The question is whether an individualism in which the self has become the main form of reality can really be sustained. What is at issue is not simply whether self-contained individuals might withdraw from the public sphere to pursue purely private ends, but whether such individuals are capable of sustaining either a public or a private life.[1]

Americans have in fact become so cynical about any form of organization, from the federal government to the PTA, that we stay clear of commitment to any of them, including such voluntary associations as ecological groups, civic improvement groups, the local Red Cross, and the neighborhood church. One reason given for the success of megachurches and metachurches is that their very size protects their members with a curtain of anonymity; people can belong to them without ever being known or recruited for service.

"Would you believe," asks Lynn Hart Roberts, executive of a large paper-processing business, "that the toughest job I have to do is try to recruit people to go door-to-door in their neighborhoods to solicit for the Heart Fund? I mean, nobody wants to help. My best friends duck when they see me coming, afraid I'll put the bite on them."

It's the same story everywhere. Everybody in America is governed by self-interest, and there are few volunteers to take on the really difficult tasks that enable major charitable institutions to keep going. "What's in it for me?" isn't merely *one* of the questions people ask in deciding what to do with their lives; for many people it is the *only* question.

The sociologists say that this individualistic attitude has developed primarily since World War II, when a country that pulled together and made daily sacrifices for the war effort relaxed and began to think about pleasure instead of sacrifice. The "Me too" frame of mind gave way in the hedonistic eighties to "Me ahead of everybody else," and some believe it is now headed into a "Me only" attitude that does not want to share anything with anyone. At present the prospects for voluntarism in the third millennium don't look very bright; some might even say they range from "bleak" to "nonexistent."

Nothing stands in the path of such unbridled individualism so challengingly as the biblical ethic that life belongs to God and we ought to live it as an offering to the divine. Jesus was unequivocal: love one another, go the second mile, turn the other cheek, do for others what you'd like them to do for you, the seed that falls into the ground and dies is the one that bears fruit. His own monumental act of sacrifice on the cross has been the touchstone across the ages for a society that idealized unselfish service to others and a willingness to suffer for outsiders and underdogs even to the point of dying for them.

The words of the great apostle have rung like a golden bell across the ages: "Let the same mind be in you that was in Christ Jesus,

who, though he was in the form of God,
    did not regard equality with God
    as something to be exploited,
but emptied himself,
    taking the form of a slave,
    being born in human likeness.
And being found in human form,
    he humbled himself
    and became obedient to the point of death—
    even death on a cross." (Philippians 2:5-8)

"For his sake," the apostle continued, "I have suffered the loss of all things, and I regard them as rubbish, in order that I may gain Christ and be found in him, not having a righteousness of my own that comes from the law, but one that comes through faith in Christ, the righteousness from God based on faith" (Philippians 3:8-9).

Everywhere people who remember earlier times bemoan the loss in our day of a spirit of sacrifice and self-commitment. Where are the great teachers who will endure anything to mold the lives of young people? Where are the physicians who care more about their patients' well-being than boats and cars and country-club memberships? Where are the ministers who cannot be lured by larger congregations and bigger salaries? Where are the law-enforcement personnel who cannot be bought by crime syndicates and influential patrons? Where are the politicians who will not succumb to the pressure and payoffs of powerful interest groups?

Whence shall come the voices calling a whole society to repentance and renewal in its ethical life? From Washington or Brussels or Tokyo or Bonn? Not very likely. From our nation's business schools? From the American Medical Association or the American Bar Association? Again not likely. From the universities and graduate schools and state houses of the nation? They are as caught up in the downward spiral of ethics as the rest of us. From Hollywood and the communications industry? That isn't even funny.

Only the church has the message that can call the nation and the world to a higher way of life, for the church is founded on the life of the One whose death on the cross has been a model for self-giving since the beginning of modern times. "This is my commandment," said our Leader, "that you love one another as I have loved you. No one has greater love than this, to lay down one's life for one's friends" (John 15:12-13). The church has not always lived up to its own message, to be sure. Its history is fractured by internal politics, dissension, and selfishness. But its ideal is as shining as ever, and holds even its members and leaders in dock for having failed to realize its own high standards.

And if ever there has been a time since the Middle Ages when the message of sacrifice and service was more needed than it is today, we would be hard put to name it. It is time for us to see the great crisis of moral life in the society around us, determine to set our own house in order, and then commence to preach the ethics of self-renunciation with a passion we somehow lost along the way. We must counter the almost universal greed and self-aggrandizement that characterize modern existence, and remind people that it isn't how many toys we collect in life that counts, or how high up the corporate ladder we climb, or how much celebrity we garner for our names and faces, but how many of Christ's little ones we comfort with a cup of cool water, how devotedly we care for the lonely, the desperate, and the ill, how faithfully we give ourselves to the task of building a better, fairer world for all, including the people who presently seem to have little in common with us.

Sermon titles should leap easily to the imagination: "Christ's Way and the World's Way," "Following Christ in a New Millennium," "Enough of Self, It's Time for a Different World!" "Dying into an Enviable Life," "Giving

Until It Hurts and Then Feels Wonderful," "Practicing the Presence by Loving the World," "Choosing the Cross When the World Offers You a Throne," "Standing for Something Before We Lose Everything," "Letting Peace Flow Down Like an Unpolluted River," "Living Lives That Count in a World That Has Forgotten How," "Restoring Sacrifice and Service as Honorable Ambitions."

The City of God

Lewis Mumford, in his classical study *The City in History*, glorified the city as one of the crowning achievements of humanity, the flowering of noble purpose, high instincts, and a desire to preserve what is best and finest in human existence. It is easy to speak that way of the city in its long and illustrious history, especially if one concentrates on the golden ages of such metropolises as Athens, Rome, Babylon, Jerusalem, Beijing, Kyoto, Paris, London, and New York. Cities have produced the most stunning cultures, the greatest collections of art, the finest theaters, the largest libraries, the best medical centers, the most extravagant restaurants and hostelries, the most glittering social life, the most brilliant dialogue and criticism, and hence the best newspapers, movies, and radio and TV programming.

But cities have also been prone to overcrowding, slums, crime, pollution, and degradation. The modern city, since the beginning of industrialization in the eighteenth century, has been particularly inclined to the victimization of the poor, the ignorant, and the elderly. Some critics go so far as to say that the contemporary city has broken down almost completely, with problems of poverty, decay, vice, and corruption that are all but unsolvable. Traffic and congestion alone have become so intense as to render many urban areas nearly untenable.

A few years ago I was in Brooklyn Heights, New York, visiting a committee seeking a pastor for a distinguished old metropolitan church. After spending the night in the home of one of the committee members, I took a subway into Manhattan to visit a friend at Union Theological Seminary near Columbia University. The subway car was so crowded that I was able to board only by being shoved on by others wishing to get aboard. We were packed in so tightly that there was no chance of falling down, for there was no room in which to fall. After my visit at Union, I caught a bus down to Fifth Avenue, where I had promised to meet another friend at his club for lunch. The club was near Fifth Avenue and Fifty-fifth Street. By the time the bus reached Seventy-fifth Street it became gridlocked in traffic, sometimes advancing a few feet when a stoplight changed and sometimes remaining stock still. When we reached Seventieth, I was already late for my appointment, although I thought I had allowed plenty of time. At Sixty-seventh Street I disembarked from the bus and made the rest of my way on foot, confident that I arrived at least twenty minutes faster than I would have if I had remained on the bus. And this was during midweek in a season of the year when New York was not particularly filled with tourists and there was no holiday!

Still, loyal New Yorkers and would-be New Yorkers defend such a way of life as "exhilarating" and "well worth it for the culture and other benefits." They may be right. Cities offer very stimulating environments in which to live and work. But the rules of sociology say that it is impossible to multiply the number of inhabitants in a given space without at the same time geometrically increasing the problems they will face with living peaceably, acquiring necessary provender, getting from one place to another with ease and comfort, and finding places of solitude and respite.

Several years ago a psychologist named John Calhoun conducted a series of experiments with colonies of rats to determine the effect on the colonies when they became overcrowded. The experiments took place in a rat pen of constant size, and food and water were provided continuously, so that the acquisition of these items did not affect the behavior of the rats. When the population of rats in the pen was held to modest proportions, the rats behaved normally and with reasonable social skills. As the population was increased, they began to develop aberrant behavioral patterns, with increased antisocial attitudes and even open fighting. By the time the pen became literally crowded with rats, they exhibited marked tendencies to viciousness, cannibalism, and perverse sexuality. Mother rats even ate their young.[2]

A major question facing the world on the brink of a new millennium is whether metropolitan existence can be made more tolerable and nourishing for the millions of people who now live here in substandard living conditions, exposed to crime and brutality on a regular basis. Those with sufficient incomes will continue to find city life intriguing and rewarding. But the others, many of them children or elderly, and often without linguistic or work skills to provide a way out of poverty and discrimination, have only a hell on earth to look forward to. They are caught in a vicious cycle of incapacity and impoverishment, crime and punishment, desertion and hopelessness, and will never be able to extricate themselves by their own decisions or abilities. Only the rest of us can make the choices that will improve their status. Only the rest of us have the means, the influence, and the understanding to break down the rat-infested walls of their ghettos and free them to live peaceful, productive lives in a world of comfort, beauty, and self-determination.

Again it is the biblical vision that is so vital to the rescue of the human situation. Even the prophets in ancient times realized that cities are far from ideal for those without the financial means or influence to enjoy them. Jerusalem, which had once been such a spiritual ideal in the minds of the early

Hebrews, had by their day become a place of political intrigue and pagan debauchery, where the poor were disregarded and the wealthy lived in blatant perversion. Isaiah and Jeremiah began intoning the need for a New Jerusalem, chastened, revised, and fully submitted to the will of God. And if we may trust the Gospels, especially the Gospel of Mark, there was considerable cynicism among Jesus and the early Christians about the reliability of cities as places of refuge and comfort for ordinary citizens; it was in the country that people were seen as being hospitable to the Savior and capable of discerning God's gift of a Messiah and a new kingdom. In the final analysis, said the writer to the Hebrews, we are looking for a city beyond all cities. "For here we have no lasting city, but we are looking for the city that is to come" (Hebrews 13:14). And the final word was left to the author of Revelation, whose vision of clashing armies and eschatological battles ended with "the holy city, the new Jerusalem, coming down out of heaven from God, prepared as a bride adorned for her husband" (Revelation 21:2).

This is the fairest city of the human imagination, declared the writer, for its builder and maker is God. Designed with foundations and walls of the greatest jewels, its streets are formed of gold. There is never any darkness in the city, for God is its light. The glory and honor of all the nations are brought into the city, and it is never defiled by anything unclean or abominable. The river of life flows through the heart of the city, with the tree of life growing fruitfully on *both* sides of the river. And the chief (and apparently only) activity in the city is the worship of God, who wipes away all tears and comforts the saints in the constant ecstasy of the eternal presence. It is the city to end all cities, a city that has become a paradigm to all city-builders until it is realized.

Here is a worthy theme for our preaching on the eve of a new millennium of human history and undertaking. Why is there hopelessness in our cities today? Because they are not built for the glory of God and the joy of their inhabitants. What does the church have to say about this? That the design for more habitable cities in the future must reflect the vision of the Scriptures. The sociologists, social workers, politicians, designers, and city-builders of tomorrow should be led by this vision, should be haunted by Christian advocates until the dream becomes more of a reality, until the cities of this earth truly reflect the glory of the city of God.

We must not be unrealistic and believe that any earthly city will ever overcome the problems of intransigence, inertia, and evil to the extent that we would wish. Like the paradisical city of Eugene Ionesco's haunting play *The Killer*, they may become technologically almost perfect and yet harbor danger and deceit because there are human beings in them and human beings are innately flawed. Yet the image of the city of God where love prevails and people exist in unity and joy is one that ought to be held before us at all times, and especially at the turn of the millennium, as a challenge to our dreaming and acting.

Imagine such sermon titles as: "A City to Top the Top Ten," "The City of Your Dreams," "A Place Where God Lives," "The City of God and the Standard of Life," "Redefining Paradise," "Reclaiming Our Cities in the Name of *the* City," "Becoming More Divine by Humanizing Our Cities," "The Master and the Metropolis," "Recovering Joy in the City," "The Light That Fills the City," "The City Without Tears," "A City Called Redemption."

Other Possibilities

These are only a few of the biblical emphases that find resonance in a time of changing millennia. There are countless others, including *separation and reunion, exile and return, blessing and cursing, work and sabbatical, betrayal and forgiveness, miracle and surprise, sowing and reaping, repentance and renewal,*

healing and restoration. "You have eyes to see," said Jesus, "can't you see?" In all of this, we are limited only by the boundaries of our imaginations.

The important thing is to read the Bible with a new eye to the time in which we read, remembering that words and ideas that might have seemed trite from overuse a few years ago become freshly and dynamically conversant under new circumstances. We should watch especially for ideas and concepts with an archetypal quality about them and stories that speak to people's hearts with force today because they have been there all along in the unconscious, waiting for amplification in a time of need.

Walter Brueggemann, in his Lyman Beecher lectures on preaching called *Finally Comes the Poet*, says:

> The preacher is called to weave an artistic connection between the text and its elusive, liberated truth, and the congregation in its propensity to hear the text in forms of reductionism. That task requires articulation of a great truth in the text that may be unnoticed reality in the congregation—unnoticed, or noticed and rejected, or routinized. Preaching makes it possible for something that has been closed to be powerfully disclosed.[3]

This is the trick with archetypal themes. The congregation *does* know them. It may not have reflected on them lately or it may have denied them altogether. But it knows them. And when the preacher begins to probe them sensitively, artistically, prophetically, especially in a time propitious for hearing, they come alive with unusual power to grip and transform. The preacher probes, there is a stirring as of some monster turning over in the deep, chaos yawns before us, and then suddenly, as if without warning, we are confronted by the very thoughts and ideas that lay inert and dormant within us all those seasons, and everything we know about life and self and God begins to assume new and arresting dimensions.

When this happens, preaching has done its work. Mystery has been reasserted, and we find ourselves before God with primordial egg on our faces saying, "Who, me?" What was closed has become powerfully disclosed again.

William L. Renfro, founder of the National Millennium Foundation, says, "The Third Millennium invites us to move from our small cycles—daily, monthly, seasonal, annual—to the grand scale of human history. From the perspective of the year 2000, Socrates and Homer are only a couple of millennial cycles away; Tutankhamen, only one more. As distant history draws closer, so also does the distant future."[4]

From such an elevated perspective, and with the great images and archetypes of scripture to draw on, we should easily do some of the greatest preaching of our entire ministries!

The Spiritual Life of the Minister at the Turn of the Millennium

The spiritual life of the minister—any minister—is problematic. It is like the sensitivity to delicate scents of the person who works in a perfumery. On one hand we are thinking and talking about spirituality all the time. On the other hand we are likely to be so familiar with it that we don't pay much attention to it, not the way we would if we were nurses or bankers or cobblers or realtors.

Miguel de Unamuno, the Spanish existentialist philosopher, once wrote a short story called "St. Emmanuel the Good, Martyr." Emmanuel was a priest who had lost his faith. But people saw the sadness in his face and thought he was an especially holy man whose heart was filled with pain for the misery of others. The worse he felt, the more people loved and appreciated him.

Fortunately God can often use our efforts at preaching and pastoring even when our hearts are not really in them. But what a pity it is if we lose the thrill and excitement of being ministers that we once felt. How much sweeter it would be if we could actually grow more and more adept at prayer and the life of grace as the years go by, and never lose the early glow of our calling.

The approach of a new millennium may strike us—as indeed it will some of our parishioners—as a capital opportunity to renew our relationship with God and deepen our inner spirits.

What happens to most of us in the parish ministry is that we become too busy about the affairs of the parish—managing a small corporation—and fail to continue with any real vigor to follow the disciplines of prayer and spirit that led us to enter the ministry in the first place. I speak a humble *mea culpa* at this point. When I was praying about whether I should leave my last pastorate for a teaching position where I would have considerably more time at my own disposal, I heard God saying in my heart, "I want my little boy back again!" I was stabbed in my conscience, for I remembered how joyously I had once walked with God along country roads and sat on outcroppings of rocks on the hillside as I poured out my heart to the Deity. My present post had driven most of the joy out of me, and I certainly had no time to walk on country roads or sit on rocks on the hillsides!

We don't mean to let our devotions go. Most of us work at them rather assiduously. But by the time we have made our daily prayers for the tired and ill and disaffected of the parish, have spent a few hours in counseling, writing letters, and composing a column for the weekly newspaper, then eaten a sack lunch with some group or committee meeting in the church hall and rushed away to make our usual rounds of the hospitals, jails, and retirement homes, stopped at home long enough to gulp down a fast meal before returning to the church for an evening meeting of some kind, and arrived at home again too spent to make much conversation or read the paper or, heaven forbid, do a little work on next Sunday's homily, we don't honestly feel very excited about the presence of God.

We know God is there. We seldom doubt that. And we feel a certain dull satisfaction at being about God's business, which we hope the parish work is. But we learn to content ourselves with less and less passion about the holy presence, and as is often the case in a long-term marriage, settle into a yoked situation where mere acceptance and stolidity take the place of stimulation and excitement. Over the years some of us become *de facto* agnostics, stumbling along in the faith primarily because we are in harness and not because we have any particular goal or destination in mind.

A former associate of mine stood looking out his living room window a few months after he retired and said, "Now that I've had a chance to review my life and work, all those piddling things I had to do to satisfy the boards and congregations in my churches, I'm not sure if any of it was worth it."

It was a terrible self-indictment. I could have cried for him. I knew hundreds of people who had benefited from his ministry and would have leaped instantly to his reassurance. But he himself had felt so little of God's spirit in it that he wasn't sure it was worth it.

The Nature of Spirituality

What is spirituality anyway? Is it the faithful saying of prayers and singing of psalms, even when one isn't sure there is anyone listening at the other end? Is it obeying the summons to ministry and plodding along in it year after year until one is released by death or the calendar? Is it refusing to listen to off-color stories and saying an unctuous-sounding table grace when it is called for? Or sitting erect and looking painfully attentive as some denominational speaker bores the pants off us?

Surely these responses aren't the right ones, even though they may serve to represent a kind of spirituality to those who are looking at us from the outside.

Spirituality—true spirituality—I think has to do more with living in constant or at least frequent awareness of God's spirit than with having a particular kind of spirit ourselves. Any spirituality we might have would after all be only reflected light, something for which we could claim no personal credit. No, it has to do with God and how attentive we are to the holy presence around us.

That rules out mere superficial devotionalism, the kind that smells in any way of posing and religiosity. We ministers are probably all a little prone to this, because we are very much aware of people watching us all the time. I knew a pastor who always knelt by his pulpit to give the pastoral prayer on Sunday morning. This struck me as extremely demonstrative, as if he were saying in a loud voice, "Hey, everybody, look at your minister on his knees! He must be a man of genuine prayer and holiness!" But I have to admit that I have probably tried to appear a little holy myself sometimes, and have hidden feelings of boredom or weariness behind a mask of piety.

Occasionally I wonder what we would be like if we carried a more immediate vision of God with us in the course of our pastoral duties. I think we would have energy shooting out our ears, we'd be so excited! We'd be like young horses that hadn't been broken, stamping and pawing and trying to burst out of the corral. Once out, we'd go galloping wildly across the fields, kicking up our heels and spinning playfully in the dust, whinnying loudly about the fire in our hearts and along our bones that won't let us rest, but makes us stampede into the very sky itself for the sheer delight of seeing what we see!

When I try to think of the times in my ministry when I have been most genuinely spiritual, I realize they usually weren't connected with my ministry at all. They were the moments when I felt most completely caught up in the divine spirit, and these normally occurred when I was in the car or on an airplane headed away from my work, or when I was on vacation, tramping along by a lake as the early-morning mist brushed my face like a soft, watery web. In other words, they were the times when I had *escaped* from the demands of ministry itself in the desperate search for rest and renewal. Then I felt the way a man must feel when he has stolen away from everyone to effect a rendezvous with a rapturous and beautiful mistress—a little guilty at the pleasure I was having, for it was away from my customary setting, but too filled with excitement and delight to care about that even for a moment.

I can only conclude, after years of puzzling over such things, that a minister's work is not actually that much more holy than the work of ordinary people who are postal clerks and stock brokers and receptionists, for despite its admirable appearance of altruism it is mostly a kind of humdrum satisfying of requirements and not a spiritually challenging campaign against death and damnation at all. Like the work of other people, it can easily interpose itself between us and God, or between us and the relaxation and leisurely spirit necessary to being alert to the presence of God. And most unfortunate of all, it tends to fool us as well as others into thinking we actually are dealing in holiness all the time, and are therefore in some way automatically spiritual, when in fact we are not as well off as they are, because we believe our own publicity releases and assume with everybody else that we are closer to God than anyone else *at the very time when we are perishing for an honest-to-goodness encounter with the holy!*

The Answer to Our Problem

What is the answer to our dilemma? I'm convinced it begins where the path to recovery starts for the alcoholic, by admitting we are not very spiritual at all and that the longer we are in ministry the worse our condition probably becomes. We have to stop confusing ministerial busyness with the life of the spirit, so that we will discover in this very realization that it is possible to feel better than we now feel, just as it is possible for everybody else in our congregations.

Once we have done this we can begin treating the ministry as the job it is—something that has become increasingly divorced in modern times from the role of spiritual mentor to the community and is now largely the work of an office manager or general caretaker. And then we will be free to feel surprised by God in a thousand ways every day of our lives, as others are surprised.

Years ago, when James D. Glasse and I were colleagues at Vanderbilt Divinity School, I was impatient with Jim's categorization of most of what we do in ministry as "paying the rent." It was a very mundane description, I thought, of the high and holy calling of the minister. But now, twenty years and two large parishes later, I apologize to Jim, because he was right. Much of what we do *is* merely paying the rent. It is as routine and unspecialized as delivering mail or stacking cans in a grocery store. And when there is too much of it to do, so that we constantly feel the pressure of not having really finished our jobs before going to bed at night, it becomes deleterious to spiritual sensitivity. More than the person in the average employment, we feel dulled and defeated by our tasks, and not a little guilty that we, who are supposed to be the spiritual gurus of the community, have not found the philosopher's stone that turns the dross of our daily affairs into golden spirituality.

Admitting that our work is not all spiritual in nature, that much of it is in fact tedious and unrewarding, will help us to set our lives in proper perspective. Yes, we are ministers, and yes, we work in the church, and yes, we spend our time serving the saints, but no, what we do is not all that ennobling, and no, it doesn't make us think about God all the time, and no, it certainly does not make us any more sensitive to the holy presence than the work that other people do. It is even possible that our working for the church actually is more enervating and debilitating than other people's work, and that we become at least mildly depressed by having to do it.

The problem is the disparity between the spiritual excitement that was once effervescing in our lives, and that probably was responsible for our entering the ministry at all, and the spiritual torpor that sets in when we have let our personal spirituality drift for a few years because we *thought* we were doing religious work and it would suffice to keep us spiritually sensitive.

I have never forgotten the day a quarter of a century ago when I attended my first seminar on prayer and meditation at Vanderbilt Divinity School. The room was crowded with men and women, many of them local ministers. We spent part of that first meeting talking about what we hoped to get out of the seminar. Many of the ministers confessed that they needed to learn to pray again.

"I've been a parish minister for thirty years," said one man. "As much as I hate to admit it, every one of those years has carried me farther and farther from the intimacy with God I once had. Sometimes now I'm not even sure if I believe in God anymore."

Once the minister admitted his problem and began to treat his job as a job, so he could separate his spiritual life from it, he began to recover his joy as a Christian. Later in the semester, he made this entry in his journal:

This afternoon I left the office about two and took a walk in the park. The dogwood trees were blooming and I sat for half an hour staring at them across the pond. I had not sat there long before I found myself talking to God, much as I did when I was a college student. We didn't talk about anything in particular. We just visited. I felt my heart filling with the wonder of things. When the time came that I had to return to the office, I hated to break it off. It was such a pleasure just to be there in the Lord's company!

He said his heart was filled with "the wonder of things." Isn't that what goes missing in the average minister's life after a few years of work? We are privileged to see and participate in so much, counseling people about the most important things in their lives, baptizing little children, marrying starry-eyed young people, dealing with grieving families, visiting the elderly, leading worship and preaching sermons, that after a while we go a little stale in our hearts and don't see the world as keenly as we once did. We're like a lot of old married folk who have eaten so many meals and watched so much TV together and slept in the same bed for so long that they don't feel any fireworks of love anymore. The once bright and brimming world has become tame and ordinary, and we are no longer alert to the glory of it.

Wonder and spirituality are closely allied. When we begin to behold the wonder again—with Roman candles going off at the sight of spring violets or the smell of fresh-brewed coffee or the sound of a child's bright laughter—we also feel the palpability of God around us, the way the presence surrounds us and laps upon us like waves upon a beach. This was the connection Gerard Manley Hopkins made that led him to write:

> The world is charged with the grandeur of God.
> It will flame out, like shining from shook foil;
> It gathers to a greatness, like the ooze of oil
> Crushed. . . .
>
> —"God's Grandeur"

And it was what Edna St. Vincent Millay must have been feeling when she penned these lines:

Lord, I do fear
Thou'st made the world too beautiful this year;
My soul is all but out of me,—let fall
No burning leaf; prithee, let no bird call.
—"God's World"

So the answer to the minister's problem of a tarnished spirituality is to recover the childlike sense of wonder in life and the world around, so that God is seen and felt everywhere in an almost unbearable closeness. The recovery itself may be effected in several ways—by taking time off, by spending minutes each day waiting in receptive prayer before God, by discovering new avenues of joy and work, by learning to play again, by undertaking a course of therapy aimed at restoring daily joy, by mastering a new language, a new skill, or knowledge of some new part of the world, or by forming exciting new relationships. And the point of discussing this here is that it may also come by an imaginative interaction with the approaching millennium, which in its pristine, as yet unformed character is capable of stimulating an incredible amount of wonder and astonishment in our hearts.

The Wonder of Time and History

There is, for example, the wonder of time and history, the sheer fact of the passing ages and what they have revealed. Standing on the brink not only of a new century but of an entire new millennium, we should have a sense of the fantastic phantasmagoria of people and events that have been and happened until now. Think of "the glory that was Greece and the grandeur that was Rome"—the Acropolis and the Coliseum, the great playwrights, artists, and architects, the philosophers and statesmen, the golden kingdoms by the sea. Think of the enchanted lands of Mesopotamia and Egypt and India—the great religions, the pyramids, the wisdom and the poetry of brilliant souls. Think of the Middle Ages, with the sweeping armies of the Moors and clashing cultures where they invaded Christendom, the brave learning of Bede and Alcuin and Charlemagne's court, and the magnificent cathedrals of Western Europe, with their soaring walls of glass and stone.

Remember the Renaissance, with its incredible burst of art, its great inquisitiveness about the past, its revival of Latin and Greek, its ferment of learning and scholarship, its fevered inventiveness, its bumptious courage in the face of plagues and fires and wars. And remember the Reformation—Luther, Melanchthon, Karlstadt, Calvin, Zwingli, Hubmaier, Munzer, Knox, and all the other doughty souls who took on not only the Holy Roman Church but an entire system and organization of life, mid-wifing the modern world. And don't forget Gian Pietro Carafa and the Oratory of Divine Love, or Benedetto of Mantua, whose *Benefits of Christ's Death* was so widely popu-lar and influential, or Ignatius of Loyola, whose Society of Jesus shaped the Catholic future as much as the Reformers shaped the movement known as Protestantism.

Imagine, either negatively or positively, all those galleons of empire sweeping this way and that across the seas, claim-ing gold and glory for Spain and Portugal and England and France and Italy, carving up continents thousands of miles from the ports out of which they sailed, and rearranging for-ever the way people thought of the world and its treasures.

Picture the inventions of the eighteenth century—the steam engine, the spinning jenny, the power loom—and how they revolutionized life in America and Western Europe, putting a new premium on fossil fuel, drawing people into cities, reshaping geography and the human psyche with wild, raw energy, necessitating trade laws, tariffs, improved bank-ing systems, stock markets, urban reform, and the Wesleys and their followers, with new methods of bringing the gospel to people in crowded cities.

With new inventions and manufacturing came deadlier and more efficient warfare, and the horrors of protracted battle—the Hundred Years' War, the American Civil War, two incredibly devastating World Wars in Europe and Britain, the last reaching around the globe to include the most formidable nations of the Orient, China and Japan, then a long, costly Cold War, punctuated by hot wars in Korea, Vietnam, Bosnia, and a dozen other places.

And there were the assaults on space—astronauts flying around the world, then to the moon, and onto landing stations among the stars. Television, with its incredible power to shape and reshape the minds, hearts, and desires of people around the world. Computers, which keep revolutionizing the way we think, store information, transact business, manage life itself. And all the advances in medicine and chemotherapy, which have turned the healing arts from guesswork and legerdemain into a marvel of precision and efficacy.

And personalities—Socrates, Plato, Aristotle, Confucius, Buddha, Moses, Julius Caesar, Jesus, Paul of Tarsus, Augustine, Benedict, Muhammad, Francis of Assisi, Joan of Arc, Meister Eckhardt, Michelangelo, Rembrandt, Henry VIII, Erasmus, Bach, Mozart, Louis XIV, Darwin, Lincoln, Dickens, Chopin, Dostoyevsky, Mark Twain, Sitting Bull, Rasputin, Woodrow Wilson, Teddy Roosevelt, Hemingway, Churchill, Stalin, de Gaulle, Reinhold Niebuhr, John Kennedy, John Wayne, Marilyn Monroe, C. S. Lewis, Picasso, Howard Hughes, Einstein, the Beatles, Minnie Pearl, Muhammad Ali, Richard Nixon, Ronald Reagan, Mother Teresa, Stephen Hawking, Mao, Madonna, Princess Diana. What a stunning array of people has crossed the stage of human existence! How many of their names most of us can recognize and recite. Glamor, power, brilliance, prestige, cunning, saintliness, diabolism—they have exhibited every quality one can think of.

Just imagine what another century, another millennium,

will bring to the earth, how their events will eventually overshadow many of the things we now consider paramount and beyond eclipse. Merely to stand at the intersection of the ages as we do should be a thrill beyond telling, an inspiration to cry out in excitement for the beauty and glory of it all. "For everything there is a season," said Qohelet, "and a time for every matter under heaven" (Ecclesiastes 3:1). Whose times and seasons are yet to come? What will the new era produce that we have not yet seen? It ought to fill us with wonder and joy merely to be here and to be able to step from one millennium into another.

The Wonder of Technology

It isn't only the people and events of the last millennia, it is also the wonderful world of technological development that should thrill us as we cross the threshold into a new age. Think about it: Aside from the wheel, fire, and a little metallurgy, technology was almost nonexistent four hundred years ago. The first successful airplane flight was in 1903. Cars didn't begin rolling off an assembly line until 1913, the year when the brassiere was designed. The zipper came into existence in 1914, and the tea bag in 1920. Vaccines began to be used in 1923, and penicillin was discovered in 1928. Scotch tape was invented in 1930, the same year when bread began to be sliced before packaging. The first computer to employ a binary code was developed in 1938. Nuclear fission didn't enter the picture until 1945. The first color television set was sold in 1951. The first heart transplant was in 1967. Space travel didn't occur until the sixties, and the lunar landing was in 1969. The World Wide Web didn't come into existence until 1990. Cloning an adult mammal didn't happen until 1997.

Someone has said that 99 percent of all inventions have been discovered in the last 1 percent of the world's history.

Imagine the innovations that will occur in the next 25 years—the next 100—the next 1,000!

Experts predict that life will be so changed in the coming half-century that none of us would recognize it if we were to fall asleep like Rip Van Winkle and wake up then. Computers will control everything in our homes, from the heat and air-conditioning to the lights, the air quality, and the cooking. We will travel in energy-saving vehicles on electronic tracks governed by computers, radar, and electric eyes. Every home will have a virtual-reality studio where we will study, conduct our business, exercise, and be entertained interactively, as if we were instantly in touch with the sights, sounds, and data of the entire globe. All our banking and most of our shopping will be done on the computer. Computers will conduct instantaneous analyses of our blood and other body fluids and give us accurate prescriptions for keeping our bodies in the best of health. Scientists will alter DNA before babies are born to eliminate cancer, deformity, and psychopathic traits. Most people will work fewer than three hours a day, and will spend much more time in travel, relaxation, and education than people now do. New materials will make possible innovative new designs in architecture, road and bridge building, and high-speed travel. There will be colonies of people living under the ocean and in outer space.

The real promise of the next century, say Adam Rogers and David A. Kaplan in a special edition of *Newsweek* devoted to the year 2000 and the power of invention, lies in a field known as *nanotechnology*. Nanotechnology is the science of rearranging molecules to turn them into almost anything we want. There are a billion nanometers in a meter, and it is in this infinitesimal world, say Rogers and Kaplan, that we shall discover the marvels of the future. Manipulating atoms, the basic building blocks of all matter, can eventually provide whatever is required, from microprocessors to skyscrapers, at a tiny fraction of what it would cost today.

Here is a kitchen scene, as envisioned by Rogers and Kaplan, half a century from now:

It's time to make dinner. But the fridge and oven are now obsolete. Instead, you go to a device resembling a microwave oven—we'll call it the Assembl-o-Tron. It has tubes running out the back that feed into a public plumbing system run by the DRM, the city's Department of Raw Materials. There's a keypad programmed with the family favorites. You hit F3 for sirloin, fries, and a salad. The Assembl-o-Tron sucks at the DRM line for a dime's worth of elemental gunk. Then, billions of microscopic robot assemblers pull and tug at the individual atoms the DRM has provided: carbon, nitrogen, hydrogen, and oxygen, maybe a few metals. In seconds, the assemblers have rearranged the elements precisely to yield the proteins and carbohydrates and whatever else makes up a good sirloin 50 years from now. Captain Kirk, it's chow time! After dinner, the garbage and fine china can be dumped back into the 'Tron for "disassembly." As long as the DRM isn't offline, cooking and cleanup are forever consigned to antiquity.[1]

The wonder of it all is breathtaking!

To some, of course, rampant technology appears to make God more and more obsolete and unnecessary. Sociologists of knowledge call it the "disenchantment" of the world. There was a time when all human beings saw the world as enchanted, with every action and event being governed by either a god or a devil of some kind. Modern science has steadily withdrawn occurrences from the sphere of enchantment, providing explanations for why they exist or happen as they do. God has thus been reduced to what philosopher of science Michael Polanyi called a "God of the gaps"—a deity who presides over the territories of ignorance and superstition not yet evaporated by the light of higher knowledge.

But thoughtful persons will not be too quick to renounce faith in the deity because of natural explanations for phenomena. As Stephen Hawking and other leading physicists have pointed out in recent years, the universe is not as simple a matter as elemental physics makes it out to be. There are eerie dimensions to things for which mere scientific explanations as they now exist cannot account. The physical world may not be as antithetical to the spiritual world as we have always assumed. God may even turn out to be the name of the unified field theory for which so many theoretical physicists are always searching.

At any rate, the technological advances of the last half-century have been mind-blowing, and those of the next half-century are likely to prove even more astonishing, even without nanotechnology. Standing at the watershed between two millennia, we should be properly amazed by looking in even one direction, much less two, for we are staring into the domain of the miraculous every day. Who would have guessed, a century or two ago, that such things are possible? And now that we live among them, our hearts should be fairly near to exploding with wonder and gratitude!

The Wonder of the Human Spirit

Perhaps the only thing more astounding than the surge of technological advances through which we are now passing is the marvel of the human spirit itself—an incredibly varied, durable, courageous, adaptive, inventive, and gifted repository of life that continues after several millennia to dazzle us all by both its failures and its triumphs.

It is hard to believe that in a building in Paris where Nazi soldiers were torturing members of the French Resistance movement a quartet of Nazis on another floor were playing Mozart and Haydn, or that the same men who oversaw the gassing of the Jews in concentration camps went home in the evening to play with their children and listen to Strauss on the radio. We are indeed an unpredictable species, given to unbelievable extremes of behavior and temperament. But poised as we are between the millennia, we must amaze ourselves with the fantastic things we are able to do. They are not mere parlor tricks, but truly incredible feats.

Think of Dostoyevsky writing that breathtaking novel *The Brothers Karamazov*. What a glorious family the Karamazovs are, and how unforgettable are the three brothers: Ivan, the intellect, the seer, the thoroughly modern man who is compelled to doubt the existence of God because of the suffering of children; Dmitri, the *bon vivant*, earthy brother who gambles, makes love, and raises a toast to life even on the eve of his departure for Siberia; and Alyosha, the saintly one, who stops his ears against the curses of his vile father, and by his love and holiness brings redemption to everyone around him. Dostoyevsky must have felt mad with genius as the speeches and actions tumbled through his head like a torrent, so that he could barely get them onto paper before falling exhausted on the table before him.

Or think of Chopin, pale, sickly, doomed to an early grave, penning his brilliant *études* and *ballades*, tone-poems of the keyboard. His was a frail spirit, one that would be judged "feminine" by the understanding of his day, and in Paris he lived with Aurore Dudevant, the famous novelist known as George Sand, a woman with drives and ambitions her contemporaries would have considered "masculine." A determined rebel, he refused to imitate the long, involved, periodic sentences of the traditional sonata, choosing instead the simple, whispered phrase. Friends urged him to attempt operatic and symphonic forms so that the world could see the range of his talent, but he chose instead to give himself entirely to the piano and the magical fragments of beauty of which he knew it alone is capable. When Liszt and Mendelssohn heard him play, they said that God was speaking through his fingers. He dressed as immaculately as a corpse in its burial clothes, for he was indeed becoming corpselike, so light and fragile that he appeared completely insubstantial; and his music was as elegant and ethereal as he was, mere shadows upon shadows of sound.

Remember Jung, whose encyclopedic mind ranged everywhere, in philosophy, science, history, art, literature, even dreams, to construct a psychology of the whole soul, of the person not only in him or herself but set within total humanity, so that it could be studied amidst all the filaments running to and from it, with life ebbing and flowing constantly, the way it does from the heart. Yet for all his knowledge he was never patronizing or contemptuous of the unlettered people around him. "Knowledge does not enrich us," he declared in *Memories, Dreams, Reflections*; "it removes us more and more from the mythic world in which we were once at home by right of birth."

Or consider Kagawa, the brilliant Japanese sociologist who spent his life trying to improve the lot of the poor in his native land. Always the enemy of slums and degradation, he moved into a tiny apartment in Shinkawa, the worst slum in Kobe, and proceeded on his own and at his own expense to care for everyone he could. He took into his room whores, thieves, alcoholics, people with contagious diseases, even murderers. One murderer was afraid to sleep at night, and Kagawa lay holding his hand so he would feel secure. Once he gave away all his clothes to a desperate man and walked around for weeks in a red kimono given to him by a woman who admired his work. Tubercular, coughing, he stood in the rain until drenched, crying out to passersby: "God is love! God is love! Not the unseen God. But where love is, there is God!"

Imagine Norma Jean Baker, who turned herself into a film star called Marilyn Monroe. A simple, breathless girl with an overpowering ambition to get into movies, she worked, drove herself, took any part, accepted any friendship until it finally happened, and she found herself a star, playing against such dazzling male co-stars as Clark Gable and Cary Grant.

She never talked; she oohed and cooed and sighed her way into a caricature of herself, and became the most notorious *femme fatale* in all of Hollywood. She married baseball legend Joe DiMaggio, and later the great American playwright Arthur Miller, both of whom thought of her as a little girl they needed to protect. She became an intimate friend of President John F. Kennedy, and sang at his birthday party. When she died of an overdose of sleeping pills, she was the woman whose initials were known all over the world, considered the very epitome of feminine beauty and sexiness.

The world is filled with fascinating people, many of whom are not at all wealthy or famous or known beyond a small circle of family and friends.

I think of Margaret, a middle-aged woman I met once on a speaking trip to Western Kentucky. Mother of a girl with a supposedly inoperable brain tumor, she read of a surgeon in Canada who could perform the needed surgery. She went to people all over Kentucky to raise the ten thousand dollars she needed to fly her daughter to Montreal and have the surgery. Even the governor made a donation. When they arrived in Canada, the immigration authorities said they couldn't leave the plane because they didn't have the proper documentation. Margaret said she was a delegate from the governor of the sovereign state of Kentucky and didn't need any other documentation. She got her daughter off the plane and into a car that took them to the hospital. The girl remained a semi-invalid from the operation and her mother cared for her day and night for several years until the girl died. Margaret had her cry and told another daughter, "Jeanie's gone to be with God, we've got to get on with our lives."

Or Railley Babcock, a salesman in Missouri, who used to be a Baptist preacher. He had read something I wrote years ago and one day came driving up our driveway in an old Ford Thunderbird. He talked like a hillbilly with his pants on fire, and reached for the stars as he gestured. When he went home—he was preaching down near San Antonio then—he began sending me copies of poems and sermons he had written, and I published some of them in a book. One day he got tired of the hypocrisy in the church and traipsed off to the hills of Missouri, where he insinuated himself into a used-car dealership and has remained ever since. But I still get phone calls from him—long, intense calls in which he pours out his soul and reads me his poetry, crisp, sourdough poetry that speaks of the hurts and joys of life, a kind of cross between Edgar Guest and Kenny Rogers.

And there's Lona Marie, a burly ex-military woman (am I right to think she was in the Marines?) who attended our church in Los Angeles. Lona Marie is an intelligent woman who writes sensible letters but has an emotional problem of some kind that is ameliorated by medication. If she forgets to take her medication she becomes truculent and unmanageable, and is ready to fight anybody who looks at her for more than a minute. She used to give me a thrill once in a while when she took on other women in the church, and sometimes she came in with a black eye or a busted nose from having gotten in an altercation on the city bus. When our son got married in the East, Lona Marie rode a Greyhound bus all the way across the country to attend, strode into the church in an expensive, colorful dress, and plopped herself down amongst the family our son was marrying into. It was her way—brusque, unceremonial, what-are-you-gonna-do-about-it?

As I said, the world is full of fantastic, colorful people. Damon Runyon and Flannery O'Connor didn't have to make them up, they were there all the time. Short people, tall people, tough people, tender people, dumb people, clever people, irascible people, dispassionate people, cynical people, gullible people. People of every size, shape, and description. People with talents for everything, from growing tomatoes to building airplanes to fixing hair. What was the slogan we used to see on T-shirts and bumpers, "God don't make no junk"? It's true. Most of us are fine stuff. We have our idiosyncrasies, such as dyeing our hair green or getting tattoos on our rumble seats or riding with one leg out the car window. But we are a rich and wonderful species, and each one of us is worth something in his or her own right. If there were ever a museum for quaint and interesting people, every one of us would belong in it.

And I am always amazed and inspired at the wonderful resiliency of people I've known. Like a young man I met at Baylor University in Texas who had had both legs amputated when he was in his early teens but led a normal life on campus. Sometimes his roommate playfully hid his prostheses and made him crawl out of bed with his arms alone and search for them, and his friends tackled him and wrestled with him on the lawn. His response to his disability? He laughed and smiled good-naturedly. "If I hadn't lost my legs I wouldn't have known how much people really care for me."

Like Mattie Nell Glasgow, a feisty old lady who had been the social director at the Waldorf-Astoria Hotel in New York City and then at the Fontaineblue in Miami. She was addicted to smoking and had a gravelly voice; but even though she had lost her husband early and had a difficult life she was full of fun and gaiety. When she was recovering from a double mastectomy and going out to her first party after the surgery, she purchased a couple of rubber duckies with squawkers in them and stuffed them in her brassiere. When any of her friends gave her a hug that night, they were startled at the sound it produced.

Surely we've all been inspired by the pluck and courage of movie star Christopher Reeve, who was injured in an accident and totally lost control of his body. But Reeve, with the help of a devoted wife and family, has kept smiling through it all, and has used his incapacity to raise funds and awareness for numerous agencies working with the physically impaired. He has even acted in and directed movies since the accident, and refuses to let being a quadriplegic turn him into a mere couch potato.

Adam and Eve were only the beginning. Now it's Rex and Regina, Ethelbert and Angelina, Satchel D. and Samantha Rose, even Bruce and Jonathan. The human race is about the most fabulous and fascinating thing in existence, and those of us who are privileged to live in the time of a new millennium, surveying the many specimens of humanity we have known and anticipating how many more there will be in the century to come, should be simply filled with awe and wonder at the spectacle of them, should fall down and praise the Creator for having made such an incredible array of lovable, likable, admirable characters.

In the words of my aunt who lived on a farm in Iowa and always saw something interesting and worth talking about when she went to town, "Some people are just hard to believe!"

The Wonder of the Earth Itself

"In the beginning," says the book of Genesis, "God created the heavens and the earth"—and then the writer promptly lost interest in the heavens and began describing the earth. And well he might, for the earth is an altogether stunning and fabulous place, from the eerie barrenness of Death Valley to the oxygen-thin heights of the Himalayas, from the snow-locked plains of Russia to the rain forests of South America, from the fjords of Scandinavia to the psychedelically colored coral reefs of Australia. What vast and interesting treasures it contains: gems and minerals, fossil fuels and precious metals, bays teeming with sea life and forests of trees and interminable fields of corn and wheat and beans.

Nobody knows exactly how old the earth is, but the evidence suggests that it has been around for millions of years and that many life-forms that once inhabited it have simply ceased to exist. Some scientists speculate that the ice age finished off the dinosaurs, while others believe that a giant comet or meteor brushed the earth ages ago, producing an enormous shock to the entire ecosystem and stopping the giant animals in their tracks, some with food still in their mouths. This, say the proponents of the comet or meteor theory, is what threw up great mountain ridges, shifting some blocks of granite as large as tall buildings a hundred miles from where they originated. Whatever happened, the earth managed to get tilted some 25 degrees off its axial course, so that it no longer spins quite evenly, helping to create many of the storms that sweep over it from time to time. And yet it twirls along, grudgingly giving up its secrets to the scientists and continuing, for all its being a tenth-rate planet in a twentieth-rate universe, to serve as our intriguing and more-than-adequate home.

Part of the miracle is in the behavior of atoms themselves, those infinitesimally tiny building blocks of which everything is made. To the naked eye they appear quite solid and dependable. A stone is a stone, and can be used to prop up a house, build a gatepost, or establish a mill. Yet the truth is, we are told, that there are trillions upon trillions of tiny particles in everything, and that these particles are racing around like mad, chasing each other in some tasteless soup, so that what appears to be solid and indivisible isn't solid and indivisible at all, except to our trusting, inexperienced minds. The wheat waving in the grain field, the granite sides of Mt. Everest, the bird feeder in the backyard, and even the seed in the feeder, are actually all of the same stuff, though in some the atoms are closer together. If an oak tree could be compressed, so that its particles were much closer together, it might be the size of a blade of grass or a poppy, though it would weigh considerably more, as its nuclei would be more numerous.

What was it the poet and visionary William Blake wrote to his artist friend George Richmond? "I sometimes look at a knot in a piece of wood until I am frightened at it." Roquetin, in Sartre's novel *Nausea*, did the same thing: he stared at the root of an old tree until he became quite dizzy at what it said to him about life and the world.

When Richard Feynman, who won a 1965 Nobel Prize for the discovery of the quantum theory of light, was asked if his knowledge of science had made the world a cold and hollow place for him, he responded that indeed it had not, that it had made it even more magical. "Now when I look at a rose," said Feynman, "I enjoy the rose for its being a rose—a lovely flower with an entrancing scent—but I also enjoy knowing about the dance of the subatomic particles inside it."

It is the same for all the sciences—physics, chemistry, astronomy, biology. What they reveal to us about the environment where we live is so wondrous that we cannot imagine its having come into being merely by accident. Somewhere, somehow, there must exist a Creator with an IQ in the millions, a Superbeing whose powers of design and engineering are absolutely staggering to the human imagination. And now, on the eve of a new millennium, with all the sciences in fast-forward mode, it is exciting beyond all speech to imagine what will be brought to light in the next few decades. Maybe somebody will develop a unified field theory that works. Perhaps, as Einstein promised, we'll learn how to put our hands through matter as if it were air. Or maybe we'll be able to transport ourselves psychically, so that we can travel from Los Angeles to London in the twitch of a nose or Cape Town to Beijing in the wink of an eye.

Of course this all sounds fanciful and impossible. But what if someone had said in the year 999 that before the next millennium was over people would fly across the oceans in great aluminum cans and even go to the moon and outer space with rockets? What if that person had predicted machines that would send instant pictures around the globe, and other machines that would act as prodigious bookkeepers, resources and sorters of information, and printers, all rolled into one? And suppose she had spoken of little pills that fight illness and disease, machines that pommel kidney stones to pieces without invading the body, lasers that can cut and heal flesh at the same time, great boxes that whir and click and make pictures of the insides of the body, mechanical constructions that can take the place of body organs? On an earth like ours, where there are such fantastic resources, it is impossible to say that anything isn't possible, only that it hasn't been discovered yet.

And then there is the sheer beauty of everything—the way different objects in the world strike us, arresting our attention, holding us as if by a magical power. A sunset viewed from a plane, so that the clouds below are bathed in reds and purples of dazzling hue. A tiny violet, growing bravely in a field of crabgrass and nettles. The face of an old woman, with skin like transparent parchment. The luminousness of a child's eyes, or the shape of its little nose. Who was it, François Mauriac, who said that in old age he could no longer bear to go to Mass, lest he look down and see the nape of a child's neck in front of him, for he could not stand the indescribable beauty of such a sight?

Think of the many artists who have seen the world with a different sort of vision and have left us clues about what they viewed. Turner, with those sublime images of sunsets and sunrises at sea. Constable, whose views of the countryside were placid and comforting, like paradise frozen in a slide. Monet, with those myopic splotches of raw color. Matisse and Picasso, who brought geometry into art, reminding us of Edna St. Vincent Millay's line that "Euclid alone has looked on Beauty bare." Chagall, whose brilliant colors suggest a child's vivid way of seeing the world. And Roy Lichtenstein and Andy Warhol, who taught us that even the comic strips and labels off tin cans can be "exploded" into gorgeous pictures to be hung on the wall.

The wonderful thing is that the great artists who help us to see the world, to differentiate colors and forms more subtly, do not really intimidate us so that we don't observe the beauty for ourselves. There are objects around us that strike each of us every day and remind us of both the profligacy and the glory of God. For example, here is a passage from a book by Michael Mayne, *This Sunrise of Wonder*, which he wrote for his grandchildren about the world they inhabit:

> This morning, as we climbed higher and higher, it was not the magnificence of the dwarfing mountains and tumbling waterfalls, impressive as they were, it was the significance of what was at our feet that claimed the eye. It was the colour and variety of the wild flowers. At first, in the low meadows, the bright yellow of dandelions and vetch, coltsfoot and arnica, the yellowish-green of spurge, the royal blue of gentians, the pink of campion and saxifrage, and the bird's-eye primrose. Higher came the mountain pansies, the tiny heartsease and white violets, forget-me-not and thyme and the just bursting Alpenrose; and higher still, the purple bee orchids and the Alpine pasque flowers, some a rich buttercup-yellow, others the shade of the crust of that thick Devonshire cream I had as a boy as a wartime treat, and can still taste. And everywhere butterflies, white ones with orange tips to their wings, brown ones with purple "eyes," tiny ones in shades of green and cobalt blue.
>
> And the crazy thing is that nature is so absurdly wasteful, so irrepressible, that most of them will grow and bloom and wither without ever being seen by human eye.[2]

That's the thing about the earth as we finish a century and a millennium. It is so full of everything, so packed with mystery and beauty, so jammed tight with miracles, that we know we have only begun to see it all, only scratched with a very tiny mark the vast surface of everything, and the coming century and millennium will carry us farther, show us more, help us to capture bits of it on film and paper and canvas, so that the eyes of millions will see more than has ever been seen, appreciate more, and be more completely dazzled. The glory of God is only beginning to be realized, and we need the time to go farther, know more, plunge into ever thicker jungles of meaning and loveliness.

What Is Spirituality?

So we come round again to the question we asked earlier: What does it mean to be spiritual? Maybe it has a lot more to do than we thought with being like Moses before the burning bush, utterly captivated by the miracle and mystery of what we behold, so that God has our attention and we are not diverted by work or pleasure or desire, so that we can hear heavenly voices whispering in our ears from everything we encounter in the world at large. If there were two persons before us, one ascetic and long-faced and pious, but with no interest in burning bushes, and the other happy-go-lucky and a bit of a rascal, and much given to turning aside whenever there is a bush aflame, we should choose to be like the second, for that is the one favored by God and is the way of being caught up truly in the spirit.

It has much to do with love and loving. Those are such misused words. We employ them to signify a kind of affection, of whatever magnitude, and a feeling of relationship. But most of us are seldom aware of the deeper meaning of the words, seldom become so caught up in them that we lose all balance and rationality.

David Steindl-Rast says it is related to blessing and being blessed, with being so filled with joy and excitement that we bless whatever is there for no other reason than that it is there. "That is our raison d'être," he says: "that is what we are made for as human beings."[3]

Maybe a good picture of love is that famous scene in *Singin' in the Rain* where Gene Kelly sings and dances in the rain, oblivious of the elements. He has found out that his sweetheart loves him and the thought possesses him completely, so that he in turn loves everything. Nothing matters to him but love. Real love is overpowering and all-consuming. It relegates everything else to the background. It fills the heart with joy and abundance, regardless of outward circumstances.

Karl Menninger, in his book *Man Against Himself*, cites the case of a Catholic chaplain in World War I, a Father Doyle, who was so much in love with God that he seemed scarcely to notice the privations and horrors of the war. In his diary, Father Doyle recorded how he returned each evening to his little bunker with both delight and fear at being alone with God, because, he said, "He is so loving there," and Doyle found it overwhelming to be carried about on the excesses of love, tossed like a little ship on the waves at sea. That is the portrait of real love, or of love truly experienced and understood. It is almost more than a human being can bear.

R. D. Laing said a wise thing about it in his book *The Politics of Experience*. It sounds like a conundrum, but it is very true. He said: "What we think is less than what we know: What we know is less than what we love: What we love is so much less than what there is; and to this precise extent, we are much less than what we are."[4] He is right, of course. "What we love is so much less than what there is," and only as we realize what there really is do we begin to become all that we might be. As we learn to sink ourselves in the sea of love, and rejoice in all that God is and has done in the world, we discover more and more of the richness of life.

True spirituality is thus much more than the form of prayer and solitude with God. It involves seeing and feeling and loving and understanding how much we are loved. And these in turn have to do with our whole lives, not with a segment of them. They are not things we switch off and on as the fancy strikes us, but things that more and more govern our lives, controlling our attitudes about everything.

Given this, there is wonderful reason for most of us to rejoice in the approach of a new millennium, for such a time as this cannot but remind us of the amazing times in which we live, and of the fantastic world that will be another thousand years old. There should be burning bushes in every alleyway and side yard, along every highway and byway of our lives. And our awareness of these flaming messengers should be contagious, so that our eyes are alight with passion and our sermons are filled with excitement.

Our congregations in the coming months should hear from us the best preaching we have ever done, and may well wonder what has worked the transformation in us. If they ask, we can tell them: We guess it had to happen in time, and this is as good a time as any.

I remember a student in one of my preaching classes a few years ago. He was preaching a very mediocre sermon in the practicum session when a secretary came to the door and called him to the telephone for an important message. We waited a few minutes for his return, and he continued the sermon. Only now the sermon seemed vibrant, commanding, full of light and joy, and the student's face reflected a kind of glory as he spoke. We were amazed at the difference.

When he had finished the sermon, the student confessed what he had learned on the telephone. His wife had just been to the doctor's office and could not wait to report to him that she was pregnant with their first child. The news made such a difference in his own level of aliveness and happiness that he returned to preach as one transformed. The sermon was unchanged; it was the same homily he had started before he left the room. But the preacher was totally altered. His mind and heart were flooded by such exuberance that it simply bubbled out and we all felt something of what was happening to him.

That's the way it is with preaching. If we are excited about the new millennium and what it can reveal of God's love in the world, our people will hear a new note in our voices and they will be excited too. They will find us changed, and the change will affect them as well.

Chapter 5

Sermons
for a
New
Millennium

Jesus Christ, the Same Yesterday, Today, and Forever?

Remember your leaders, those who spoke the word of God to you; consider the outcome of their way of life, and imitate their faith. Jesus Christ is the same yesterday and today and forever. Do not be carried away by all kinds of strange teachings; for it is well for the heart to be strengthened by grace, not by regulations about food, which have not benefited those who observe them. We have an altar from which those who officiate in the tent have no right to eat. For the bodies of those animals whose blood is brought into the sanctuary by the high priest as a sacrifice for sin are burned outside the camp. Therefore Jesus also suffered outside the city gate in order to sanctify the people by his own blood. Let us then go to him outside the camp and bear the abuse he endured. For here we have no lasting city, but we are looking for the city that is to come. Through him, then, let us continually offer a sacrifice of praise to God, that is, the fruit of lips that confess his name. Do not neglect to do good and to share what you have, for such sacrifices are pleasing to God.

Obey your leaders and submit to them, for they are keeping watch over your souls and will give an account. Let them do this with joy and not with sighing—for that would be harmful to you.

Hebrews 13:7-17

I t actually happened in church, during the children's sermon. The minister was young and confident. In fact, he simply exuded confidence, like the coach of a team that hasn't been defeated all season. "Now children," he exclaimed with enthusiasm when they were assembled in front, "we're going to do something a little different today. I want five of you to line up here [he didn't wait for volunteers, but started lifting children up by the forearms] and I'm going to show you something." He whispered into the ear of the first child, then said aloud, "Now whisper the same thing into the ear of the person next to you." He had each child whisper to the next, passing along the message.

"Now," he declared, "I'm going to show the congregation what I whispered to the first one of you." He held a poster aloft bearing the message: "Jimmy kissed Brenda under the willow tree."

"What I want to teach you today," he continued, "is the way gossip gets distorted as we pass it from one person to another. Then we'll talk about telling the gospel to others, and how important it is to do that instead of gossiping." He was very loud and upbeat about it, and the entire congregation was following with interest.

"What's your name?" he asked the fifth child in line. "Billy," said the little boy. "Billy," he said, "I want you to tell us what this young lady next to you whispered in your ear." Billy looked frightened and stupefied.

"Okay," the minister said in a loud voice, "that's okay, Billy. I was a little scared the first time I spoke in public too. I'm going to ask your friend to tell you again, and this time you remember it and repeat it for the rest of us, okay? And we'll see how gossip gets twisted around when it is passed from person to person."

The little girl next to him leaned over and whispered into his ear again.

Billy looked at the minister and in a voice clearly audible throughout the sanctuary repeated the message exactly as it was printed on the poster: "Jimmy kissed Brenda under the willow tree."

I actually felt sorry for the young minister. He had been too confident of how his little experiment would turn out. Now he was flushed and embarrassed. But he didn't let that stop him from drawing the conclusion he had planned from the beginning. "All right," he said, "gossip *usually* gets all changed as it is passed from one person to another, although you are an extremely clever group of children. What I want you to remember is that we ought never to gossip. Instead, as Christians, we should tell people the gospel. Can you remember that? Don't gossip, but tell the gospel."

I don't know if anyone else in the sanctuary was thinking what I was thinking, but to me that innocent and ill-fated little exchange with the children raised a far more profound question than the young minister had intended to raise. That was, What about the gospel itself and how it has become distorted as it has been told and retold through the ages? If gossip gets distorted, doesn't the gospel get distorted too?

Surely it does. Otherwise there wouldn't be so many kinds of Christianity around today, each insisting on its particular view of faith. There are, for example, the sacramentalists and the conversionists. Sacramentalists believe that God is mediated to us in many forms and that we must remain open to these various ways, which range from receiving the bread and cup in church to seeing God in art and nature and everywhere else. Some sacramentalists go to the extreme, rejecting even the bread and cup as symbols too limited to be meaningful, and profess to find God in other religions as well as Christianity. Conversionists, on the other hand, insist that the Christian community has been given specific instructions about what we must do to be saved and that we must follow these to the letter or be lost. And then there are those who believe that we should above everything else receive the Spirit of God, and that the Spirit manifests itself in tongues-speaking and the power to heal the sick. And there is a variety of Spirit-filled religion that says snake handling is a test of our faith, that if we are going to take the Bible seriously then we must pay attention to a little verse in the last chapter of the Gospel of Mark which says that those who follow Jesus "will pick up snakes in their hands" (Mark 16:18).

What is the truth? How much of what we hear about the gospel is a distortion passed down through the ages? Leslie Weatherhead wrote in *The Christian Agnostic* that what has happened to the Christian message reminds him of a legend about a shepherd's pipe that was supposed to have once belonged to Moses, the great Hebrew leader. Sometime after Moses' death, it was decided that the pipe was altogether too plain and unattractive to have been Moses', and so it was embellished with gold. A few centuries later, some enthusiastic Jews decided to make it even more attractive, and overlaid the gold with further "improvements" in gold and silver. Thus the pipe became extremely handsome and impressive—but it had lost its wonderfully pure and simple musical tone and could no longer be played.

We're nearly ready to enter a new millennium of the earth's history. How many distorted understandings of the gospel will we carry along with us when we do? I don't know about you, but I'd like to move into the new millennium clean. I'd like to leave behind as many superstitions and distortions as I can, and not have them cluttering my mental and moral landscape.

Jesus, according to the scripture we read, is always the same. He was the same yesterday, he is the same today, and he will be the same tomorrow. Jesus doesn't change.

Or does he? Apparently the early Christians saw him as a man anointed by God with a special message and mission, and then raised up by God when he had been crucified. Then there was a great conference at a place called Nicaea several centuries later in which the nature of Christ was debated and it was decided that he was actually God—even though he himself had once said to a man, "Why do you call me good? No one is good but God alone" (Luke 18:19). And from that decision developed an elaborate medieval theology centered on the idea that people who ate the bread and drank the cup were eating and drinking God. The Reformers of the sixteenth century took issue with this, calling it magic and superstition, and reasserted the human aspects of Jesus. During the Enlightenment of the eighteenth century, Jesus was declared to be only a good moral leader, and successive biographies of him tried to explain away the miraculous occurrences in the Gospels, saying they were nothing more than hoaxes perpetrated by the early church. The Social Gospel movement of the twentieth century again asserted that Jesus was a great moral leader, and emphasized his good works on behalf of the poor and outcast of society. The Jesus Movement of the sixties and seventies saw him as a kind of mystical figure who is always present to his followers. That led in turn to the insistence of fundamentalists and conservatives in the last few decades that Jesus is both Lord and God. We cannot predict how he will be seen in the twenty-first century, for even a decade or two can introduce enormous changes in the way we see things.

Maybe it is the same with Jesus as with Moses' pipe and the gospel. Who is he really? We tend to see him from different angles, depending on our own backgrounds and experiences. What does the Bible mean when it says he is "the same yesterday and today and forever"?

To understand what the writer of the Letter to the Hebrews was saying, it is important to survey the letter itself. Otherwise we will merely read into the phrase whatever we want to, depending on our individual experiences. The overall thrust of the book of Hebrews is an appeal to Jewish Christians not to desert their new faith because of persecution or difficulty. Jesus, it says, is both the perfect sacrifice for our sins and the true high priest. Had the author been addressing a non-Jewish group, he might have chosen a different emphasis. But he knew that Jews would understand the allusions to the sacrificial system in the Jewish faith, and to the importance of the high priest in that system. And then, having painted this portrait of Jesus as both sacrifice and priest, the author talks a great deal about the urgency of having faith, of trusting the things that can't be seen and verified at this point, and gives a list of examples of those who took God's promises on faith. The list includes almost everyone of significance in the history of the Jewish faith.

This then is the context for understanding what the writer meant by "Jesus Christ is the same yesterday and today and forever."

What can anyone do to us? asks the writer. "Remember your leaders"—those who led you into the Christian understanding. "Consider the outcome of their way of life." That is, couldn't you bear whatever happened to them? Were they cowardly in the face of persecution and discomfort? "Imitate their faith." Behave as they did.

Then comes the statement: "Jesus Christ is the same yesterday and today and forever." He was not one Christ to them and another to you. If he was important enough to demand their loyalty, to call them out of their old faith into the new one, then he is important enough to demand yours as well. He does not alter from one year to the next. He will always be the Christ who commands our devotion and faithfulness.

Ah, that's a little different, isn't it? It doesn't mean that Christ doesn't change in the eyes of those who perceive him from generation to generation. It simply means that he is big enough and important enough—he is the same Christ who commanded the original apostles to risk their lives in the propagation of the faith—to be the Lord of your faith as well, in whatever time you live.

You say, That doesn't really solve any problems about the

nature of Jesus, does it? You're right, it doesn't. It isn't a theological commentary on the nature of Christ's person,
whether he was an exemplary leader or "very God of very
God," as those who hold to a high Christology like to say. It
doesn't tell us whether we ought to handle snakes or speak in
tongues. It simply says, "Christ is our leader, as he has always
been, and he is worth following—even worth dying for, if it
comes to that. So don't give up on the faith."

But maybe that is a message we need to hear as we enter
the new millennium. Maybe we need to be reminded that
Jesus is still the one through whom God has been revealed to
us, and that therefore we should be following him, whatever
our theological and moral understandings of him. Maybe it
even means that we Christians ought to be more accepting
and tolerant of one another, regardless of how we see Jesus
and his nature and work, for he is after all our Lord, the one
before whom we all bow down in humility and devotion.

The next millennium will put Christians to the test in
many ways, all over the globe. In some places there will be
persecutions for the faith. In others, like our own country
today, there will be such laxity that people simply fall away
from the faith out of boredom and inattentiveness to what
they believe. But the message of this ancient book will still
be important: "Jesus Christ is the same yesterday and today
and forever." We ought to stand up and be counted as his followers. We ought to be faithful—for that is part of what it
means to have faith.

I heard this story from a Catholic priest on a TV show.
The host had been questioning him about the nature of
Jesus, and he had been careful not to say anything that would
allow his theology to be pigeonholed and thus dismissed.
Instead, he said he wanted to tell about something that had
actually happened.

It was about a woman who went to her priest and said she
thought her father was dying; would the priest please come by

to see him? He promised he would when he was in the neighborhood. "I'm sometimes out to run to the store," said the woman. "I'll leave the door open. If there's no answer to your knock, just go on in. You'll find my dad's room in the back."

One day the priest stopped. There was no answer to his knock, so he went on through to the father's room. When he got there he found a chair pulled up close beside the bed. "Ah, you must have been expecting me," said the priest. No, said the man, the chair hadn't been put there for the priest. "I'll tell you, father," said the man, "I'd been having trouble praying. But a friend said if I would put a chair there for the Master, and pretend he was sitting there, I could talk to him more naturally. So I placed the chair there and tried it, and it really works." "That's fine," said the priest. "Anything that helps."

A few days later the woman came to the priest and told him her father had passed away. The priest expressed his sympathy and asked if her father had died easily. "Oh, I think so," she said. "A little while before, he had called me in to show me something in the funny papers, and we both had a laugh over it. Then I went out to the store to get some milk, and when I came back he was dead."

"I'm glad it was easy," said the priest.

"There was just one odd thing," said the woman.

"Oh?" said the priest.

"Yes," she said. "Apparently he had pulled a chair over to the bed and was struggling to get into it or to use it to stand up, because when I found him he had pulled his head and shoulders over to the chair and died with his head in it."

He will *always* be our leader, whatever the century or millennium, for he is the same *yesterday*, in the time of the great apostles; *today*, when you and I are thinking about him and how we should be committing ourselves to him; and *forever*, even in the new millennium and beyond; for he is the Christ of God and the Savior of the world.

Nothing New/ Everything New

What has been is what will be,
and what has been done is what will be done;
there is nothing new under the sun.

Ecclesiastes 1:9

So if anyone is in Christ, there is a new creation: everything old has
passed away; see, everything has become new!

2 Corinthians 5:17

"What has been is what will be, and what has been done is what will be done," says the writer of Ecclesiastes; "there is nothing new under the sun."

That isn't very welcome news as we approach a new millennium, is it? When we have just made it through another madcap decade filled with sadness, illness, death, poverty, injury, loss, terrorist acts, and war, we want something new. We long in the deepest parts of us for something new. I reread the Christmas letters we received this Christmas, which is something I always do after the Christmas rush is over, and I was struck by how many people said, after detailing the bad news of what had happened in their families last year, "We hope the new year and the new millennium will be different!" So it is very sobering to be told in scripture itself, "Forget it, nothing ever changes."

Who was the writer of Ecclesiastes, and what right did he have to make such a pronouncement? Contemporary scholars usually refer to him as Qohelet, which is the Hebrew name of the book and may or may not have been a real name at all. The word doesn't appear anywhere else in the Old Testament, but seems to be related to the Hebrew word *qahal*, or "assembly." Qohelet may have meant something like "preacher" or "speaker in the assembly." Qohelet's book was written when the man was very old as a guide to moral understanding for others. He tells how, as a young man, he followed the usual vices of the young but found no comfort in them. Then, as he grew older, he saw what a cyclical thing human experience is—it goes round and round, repeating itself in all human beings in every place. This led him to conclude that all human life is mere vanity. "Vanity of vanities," he says, "all is vanity!" What goes around, comes around. There is nothing new under the sun.

Depressing, isn't it? We would like to be liberated from the cycle, especially as we approach a whole new millennium.

But then we hear this other voice from scripture, in a part of the Bible we call the *New* Testament. It says: "If anyone is in Christ, there is a new creation: everything old has passed away; see, everything has become new!" *Everything* has become new. The first writer said *nothing* is new. The second says *everything* becomes new.

What's going on here?

The answer is that the writer of the second message was the apostle Paul. Paul had experienced life as vanity too. But then Paul met Christ on the road to Damascus, and suddenly the vanity was transcended. The old Paul, who had been struggling so hard with life, who had found it impossible to be what he wanted to be alone, became a new Paul. He saw everything with a new eye, felt everything with a new heart, undertook everything with a new eagerness! His old life had passed away and everything had become new!

114

And the beautiful thing about this transformation was that it wasn't anything Paul himself did. He didn't work for it at all. He didn't make it happen. It happened *invasively*. That is, it entered his life from outside and changed everything. It was a glorious, life-altering experience.

Wouldn't it be wonderful to have that happen to you? I have a friend in a prison in Tennessee. I have never met him, but the chaplain is a friend of mine—a former student actually—and told him about me, so he wrote to me and I wrote to him. We have been corresponding for several years now. My friend writes about many things, but the one theme that appears consistently in all his letters is his desire to get out of prison. I can understand that, can't you? Well, what if one day some special person were to walk through that prison and tap my friend on the shoulder and say, "You are free to go now, you can just get out of here!" It would seem like a miracle, wouldn't it? It would seem almost unbelievable!

That's essentially what the good news of Christianity is about. It's about someone walking into the prison where we live and saying, "You're free to go now. Get out of here! You thought you were condemned to an endless cycle of failure and disappointment and unhappiness, but there is something new. Christ has come into your life and transformed all your possibilities. You thought there was nothing new; now everything is new!"

Now, you're clever enough to understand how the newness comes. We aren't suddenly whisked out of our old worlds, the way Scrooge was carried away by those wonderful ghosts in *A Christmas Carol*. We are left right in the worlds where we were, looking at the same old scenery and the same old people. But everything *looks* different to us!

That's right. The change has come about in the way we see everything, the way we relate to it, the way we deal with it.

That's the way it was with Paul. He didn't suddenly find

himself in paradise, with angels feeding him champagne and chocolate cake and strawberries. He was still in a world of magistrates and marketplaces, diseases and discomforts, drafty rooms and dusty roads, agriculture and economics. But the world looked completely different to him. The Bible says he was struck blind by Christ, and then, when God's messenger came and touched him, the scales fell off his eyes. I'm not saying he wasn't really blind; only that what happened to him was a miracle of seeing everything in a new way. The Christians didn't look like his enemies anymore. The law didn't look like such a big deal. His future as an advocate of the law looked bleak indeed! And everywhere he looked, he saw opportunities for Christ.

It was the same for all those early Christians—Peter, James, John, the lot of them. After Christ came into their lives, everything looked different.

The world hadn't changed, but they had.

Do you remember the story they used to tell about the orator who was preaching about communism at Hyde Park Corner in London, the place where anybody who wants to speak on any subject is free to do it? He was expounding the virtues of communism and what it could do for the world. A little crowd had gathered to listen to him, and there was a poor, shabby fellow on the front row in a very worn old overcoat. Reaching the high point of his fervor, the speaker pointed at the fellow in the old coat and exclaimed: "Communism, my friends, will put a new coat on that man!"

It seemed a reasonable attraction for communism until a Christian gentleman who was standing at the back of the crowd hollered out, "That may well be, my friend, but Christianity will put a *new man* in that coat!"

Nothing new, everything new.

How does it happen? I said that it is invasive, that it comes to us from outside ourselves, it isn't something we work up for ourselves. How does the newness come upon us?

It usually happens very simply. Very simply indeed, as it did in the case of a man with whom I recently had lunch. He is the president of a large insurance company in Birmingham, and a friend wanted me to meet him and hear his Christian testimony.

I said, as we were eating our salads, "I understand you have had a wonderful Christian experience. Would you mind telling me about it?"

He said, "Well, it wasn't very dramatic, but I am happy to tell about it. It was sometime after the Watergate affair, when President Nixon was brought down in humility. I was not a Nixon fan, but I was fascinated by Watergate and the whole process that destroyed a presidency, and I was reading everything I could about it. Somebody gave me a copy of Charles Colson's *Born Again*, the autobiography in which Colson talked about his part in the Nixon tragedy and what happened afterward in his own life. I was sitting in my den reading the book one night, and read about Colson's conversion—the episode where he sat in his car in the rain and cried. I had gone to church all my life, but didn't feel that I had ever been converted. So I put the book down in my lap and closed my eyes and prayed. I said, 'Dear God, I would like to be converted like that,' and I was. I felt different from that moment on."

"That was the first thing," said the man. "Then I had a second experience. Someone else gave me a book by a Pentecostal about being baptized by the Holy Spirit. I had never given a thought to such a thing. But as I read about the great joy that came to the author from being baptized by the Spirit, I laid the book down and prayed, 'Dear God, nothing like this has ever happened to me. I would like to be baptized by the Holy Spirit.' And I was!"

I asked him if he ever spoke in tongues. "Sometimes," he said, "but never in public. When I'm praying, I often end with a short time of tongues-speaking, when the Spirit speaks through me and in my behalf. But that isn't what's important about being baptized by the Spirit. Being baptized by the Spirit has to do with feeling the sense of deep joy God wants to give us, with knowing that, whatever happens in the world, we are in God's hands."

You couldn't get any simpler than that, could you? He merely realized he hadn't been converted, and prayed to be converted. He realized there was a baptism of the Spirit, and knowing he had never had it, prayed to receive it. He didn't *do* anything to change his life except pray to be changed. And he was changed. Everything was made new for him.

"What about the joy of the Spirit?" I asked him. "Do you feel that you have it?"

"Oh yes!" he said, his face lighting up. "My whole life has been different since I experienced it. I approach my work differently. I look at my family differently. I feel differently about my mortality. Everything was changed when I had those experiences."

This doesn't mean poor old Qohelet was wrong. He was a very wise man. He saw the vanity of the world. But Qohelet had a disadvantage. He lived before Christ. He didn't understand, as some of the prophets did, what a change Christ's coming into the world would bring. He said nothing ever changes. But he didn't realize that, in Christ, everything changes.

Which brings us back to you and me and the new millennium. We hope the next century will be better than the last. We would like for a lot of things to be different. And the promise of the gospel is that they can be. But not through the world's being different. Through *our* being different, *our* seeing things with new eyes, *our* living our lives differently.

The world will probably go on pretty much as it has, only wilder and faster than ever. There will be many more medical and technological discoveries in the coming decades.

Maybe there'll be a cure for cancer and even a cure for the common cold. Maybe there'll be weekend travel to the moon one of these days, or at least cars that operate on nuclear energy and don't break down so often. Maybe there will be computers that function solely on voice commands, so that even the tehnologically illiterate will know how to work them. But the really great advances, the ones that will make everything seem new and different for us, must be made in our own hearts. That's where our work is cut out for us. That's where the true differences in the next century will come.

And it isn't really hard. It's only a matter of accepting what God has already done in Christ. God has given us a new life, a new way of seeing. And, like the man who realized he didn't have it, all we have to do is ask for it.

Sermon 3

The Church for the New Millennium

I am the true vine, and my Father is the vinegrower. He removes every branch in me that bears no fruit. Every branch that bears fruit he prunes to make it bear more fruit. You have already been cleansed by the word that I have spoken to you. Abide in me as I abide in you. Just as the branch cannot bear fruit by itself unless it abides in the vine, neither can you unless you abide in me. I am the vine, you are the branches. Those who abide in me and I in them bear much fruit, because apart from me you can do nothing. Whoever does not abide in me is thrown away like a branch and withers; such branches are gathered, thrown into the fire, and burned. If you abide in me, and my words abide in you, ask for whatever you wish, and it will be done for you. My Father is glorified by this, that you bear much fruit and become my disciples. As the Father has loved me, so I have loved you; abide in my love. If you keep my commandments, you will abide in my love, just as I have kept my Father's commandments and abide in his love. I have said these things to you so that my joy may be in you, and that your joy may be complete.

This is my commandment, that you love one another as I have loved you. No one has greater love than this, to lay down one's life for one's friends. You are my friends if you do what I command you. I do not call you servants any longer, because the servant does not know what the master is doing; but I have called you friends, because I have made known to you everything that I have heard from the Father. You did not choose me but I chose you. And I appointed you to go and bear fruit, fruit that will last, so that the Father will give you whatever you ask him in my name. I am giving you these commands so that you may love one another.

John 15:1-17

A little girl went to bed one night with all her clothes on. When her mother came up to tuck her in, she expressed surprise. "What in the world are you doing, honey?" she asked. "You've never done this before." "It was what our teacher said," replied the little girl. "What was that?" asked the mother. "Our teacher said that things are changing so fast now that there isn't any time to get ready for them. I thought if I kept my clothes on I would be ready."

The world *is* rapidly changing. Half a century ago, few of us had heard of television; now it is the predominant form of communication on earth. We knew nothing of computers; yet now our lives are being revolutionized by their existence. We had no understanding of DNA, that remarkable little string of cells in our bodies that makes the decisions about the replication of all our other cells; today we are told that scientists will soon be able to alter our DNA, perhaps eliminating cancer and Alzheimer's and other debilitating diseases, and, in the bargain, producing cells that are superintelligent and superathletic. If Rip van Winkle were alive today and in need of another nap, he would not have to sleep for twenty years to find everything different. A few days, or even a few hours, would be quite enough. And he *did* sleep with his clothes on.

It isn't any wonder, given such an era of explosive transition, that many of us are deeply concerned about the changes occurring in Christendom and long for the churches we knew in quieter, less turbulent times. The little church in the wildwood was a very comforting institution, and the old church on the corner wasn't bad either. Now churches are being whiplashed by all kinds of altering conditions—new translations of the Bible, the metamorphosis of doctrinal and social issues, the breakup of community, the disintegration of the traditional family, and horrendous economic pressures—and Darwin's creed about the survival of the fittest, once so abhorrent to many Christians, can be aptly applied to them.

We don't know what the future church will look like—what kind of architecture it will develop, what kind of music it will finally settle on, what kind of social and theological issues it will wrestle with, what kind of posture it will assume in the world. But we do know what its agenda ought to be. That agenda has been there from the beginning, in the words Jesus spoke to his disciples before his death. Biblical scholars refer to John 14–16 as Jesus' Farewell Speech, a genre whose pattern was set in Israel by the last speeches of such eminent figures as Moses and David and Elijah. These chapters are Jesus' last will and testament—what he wanted the disciples to remember most faithfully in the years ahead—and they give us an ample pattern of what he expected of the beloved community, the church, as long as it exists in the world. We don't have time now to deal with the entirety of the three chapters. But the crux of them is in the first part of chapter 15, a section that Jesus appears to have spoken on the way to the Garden of Gethsemane. And there are three emphases in that section, three descriptions that will always characterize the true church of Jesus Christ.

First, Jesus used the analogy of the branch remaining in the vine to receive its nutriment and continue to bear fruit, and ordered the disciples, "Abide in me as I abide in you" (John 15:4). That is, "Continue to turn to me for all your understanding, nourishment, and direction, and I will continue to bless you with all of these things."

Does it appear too simplistic to say that the church in every age is built around the person of Jesus Christ? Yet we know that down through the centuries there have been many institutions claiming to be the church that have exhibited little proof of being in communion with the humble Galilean who cast his lot with the poor and despised: Churches of great wealth and prestige lavishing expensive gifts on themselves while people starved in the alleys around them. Churches of social preeminence erecting their luxurious facilities among great homes and country clubs while neglecting the ghettos of poverty, crime, and disease in their larger communities. Churches with snobbish intellectual pretensions that disdained honest working people and those who had no grasp of simple wit or theological subtlety. Churches with invincible programs of belief and doctrine and with zero tolerance for those who did not agree with them at every point.

How foreign Christ must have felt in the vicinity of any of these churches! Surely he has wept over them as he wept over Jerusalem, crying, "Oh churches, churches, how often I would have gathered you as a hen gathers her chicks under her wing, and you would not!"

And how ashamed he must be of some of us today, with our radical divisiveness, our splitting of the church into liberal and conservative, doctrinal and social, missionary and nonmissionary, charismatic and noncharismatic, ethnic and nonethnic, intellectual and nonintellectual, while the world around us—*his little ones*—perishes for lack of food and guidance and technical assistance. "Abide in me—*continue in me*—and I will continue in you." And we have not abided, have we? We haven't continued in him. We don't listen to him. We listen to every other voice around us, all the strident, belligerent, discordant, opinionated, persuasive voices in the world, but we don't listen to him.

I remember the last meeting of the board of trustees I attended as pastor of a large metropolitan church. A large, *wealthy* metropolitan church. I had made a simple request, that the church rent some portable toilets and place them in our parking lot for the use of the many homeless people in our neighborhood. Most of us don't think about it, but the homeless have a major problem finding places to use the bathroom. Many restaurants in our neighborhood had hired guards to turn them away from using their facilities. They were forced to seek relief among the trees and bushes of the park, where they were often rousted by the police for indecent exposure. A few portable toilets wouldn't solve all their problems, but they would have been a welcome assistance.

I could not believe the intensity of the argument that ensued, or the variety of reasons adduced for our not providing this simple, affordable luxury for the poor. Some of the arguments were sensible, and I can recall them: Word would get out that our church had free bathrooms, and we would soon have half the homeless population of the city encamped around us. We had a day school at the church with 450 students. What if one of the people we attracted molested a child or a teacher? We would have a major lawsuit on our hands. The women of the church would not want to use our parking lot and have to pass among all the dirty, unkempt homeless people to come to meetings at the church. And on and on it went. Good reasons, sound reasons, not to do it.

But where was Jesus in all of this? What would his position have been? Remember "Whoever gives a cup of cool water..."? Ironically, the Savior who gave everything for those who didn't deserve it was succeeded, in this instance at least, by an institution that didn't want to risk a lawsuit.

It isn't easy, abiding in Jesus. But it is the only way we shall be church.

The second thing he said was: "Love one another as I have loved you." Abide in me and love one another.

We're surely better at that, aren't we? We may not have abided in him very well, but loving one another hasn't been a problem. We all have so much in common in the church. We're like-minded folks. We look after our own. We take care of our wounded.

Or do we?

Why is it someone has said, "The church is the only institution in the world that shoots its own wounded"?

Does that mean we don't love sinners the way we're supposed to? That we love *only* those who are just like us, who look and dress like us, who profess to believe just what we believe? That we impose tests and restrictions on those we intend to love? That we want to get rid of the ones who aren't like us and don't agree with our ideas about life and politics and education and religion?

I was teaching a course at the Claremont School of Theology, in California, and a young woman who was a candidate for the ministry asked if she could meet me in a private conference. She was troubled, she said, by something she had learned. Late one Saturday night she remembered that she needed some papers from the church where she was an intern to complete her preparation for Sunday morning, so she drove into the church lot, intending to let herself in with the key she had. But she saw a light in part of the building, and approached stealthily. Through the window, she saw a man and woman who had been trying for months to get rid of a pastor they didn't like. They were trashing the Sunday school rooms, strewing paper about, writing on the boards, and disarranging the furniture. "They had been complaining to the church board," said the young woman, "that the pastor wasn't properly overseeing the janitors and insuring the good appearance of the property. And there they were sabotaging his efforts!" Her problem was that she didn't know if she could go into the ministry of a church where people in the congregation behaved that spitefully.

Now, I know nobody hearing this sermon would do that sort of thing. But if you're ever tempted to, remember that young woman's dilemma. And remember Jesus' saying that we are to love one another as he has loved us. "No one has greater love than this," says the text, "to lay down one's life for one's friends" (John 15:13). What if that couple in the church that night had sat down and thought about this? That they were to love the pastor they didn't like, and remember that Jesus had loved them so much he had laid down his life for them? Do you think it would have caused them to behave differently?

When I try to focus on someone who has really loved the way Jesus said, I keep thinking of John and Larry. John was a paraplegic in a church I pastored. He had had toxic plasmosis as a teenager, and by the time I knew him was reduced to a distorted, skeletal figure in a wheelchair who could no longer talk in anything more than rasps and grunts. Sometimes in church, if I said something John thought was humorous, he emitted a loud, hideous laughter, usually a minute or two after the humor had passed, and disconcerted everybody sitting near him. Larry was a commercial artist who had met John one night at a church supper. John's parents were caring for him then, but the task was becoming more than they could manage. Larry offered to help by taking John for a few hours at a time. Then he began taking him for weekends. And when I came to know them, Larry had quit his job and was working independently at home so that he could care for John full-time.

Once I expressed to Larry my great admiration for him, and the sacrifice he was making for John. "Oh, it's no sacrifice," he said. "Whenever I look at John, I see Jesus, and I can't help loving him."

"Abide in me." "Love one another as I have loved you." And finally: "Go and bear fruit, fruit that will last" (John 15:16). We are to abide in him, and love, in order that we may bear fruit. Not ordinary fruit, fruit that will perish in a few days. But fruit that will last and last forever.

What did Jesus mean by that? "Go and bear fruit." He had spoken about being the True Vine, and our being the branches, and said that if we remained in him we would be able to bear fruit. But what kind of fruit, aside from the fact that it will last?

Could there possibly be a connection between this passage and the story of the Garden of Eden? Jesus was then on his way with the disciples to the Garden of Gethsemane, the garden where he would submit himself to the Father's will and offer himself for crucifixion. Was he thinking about the Garden of Eden too, and what it had all come to? Adam and Eve were supposed to abide in God, continuing in a blessed relationship, but they didn't; they disobeyed and hid from God's presence. They should have found it easy to love one another, but apparently they didn't; they blamed one another for their disobedience, and later their son Cain, in a jealous rage, slew their son Abel. And God told them to "be fruitful" and to "multiply." Was this speech of Jesus modeled in any way on the story of the first man and woman, and how they had failed to remain in God? They had been fruitful, had had children and populated the earth. But what did Jesus mean when he told the disciples to bear fruit that would last? Is it related to abiding in him and loving one another?

Maybe Paul understood what it was about when he talked about "the fruits of the Spirit," in his letter to the Galatians. Do you remember? He spoke of "the works of the flesh"—fornication, impurity, idolatry, strife, jealousy, anger, quarrels, dissensions, factions, and all of those things (Galatians 5:19-21). Those are what we have when we don't abide in Christ and love one another. And then he spoke of "the fruits of the Spirit": love, joy, peace, patience, kindness, generosity, faithfulness, gentleness, and self-control (Galatians 5:22-23).

"Go and bear fruit that will last," Jesus said. Are these the things he meant? That we can transform the world with these things? That they have a beautiful, eternal quality about them? That they are what God wants from us, has *always* wanted from us? That they are what will make the church attractive to the world around us, and will spill out of our churches and into our neighborhoods and communities and nations until the whole world is the way the Garden of Eden was supposed to be?

Perhaps you are familiar with Randy Frazee's Spiritual Fitness Assessment test. Frazee is a young minister in Dallas. Disappointed that the people in his church didn't appear to be different in any way from the people in the community beyond the church, he developed his test for spiritual fitness around the fruits of the Spirit described by Paul. There are sixty statements on the test, and the person taking the test responds to each statement on a six-point scale ranging from "Strongly agree" to "Strongly disagree."

Here are some of the statements: "I give away my money to serve and help others." "I am free from worry and anxiety." "I am patient when I have to wait on people, or for things to happen." "I allow people the room to make mistakes." "I believe that everything I am or own belongs to God." "I have no habits or addictions that have power over me." "I put matters into God's hands when I am under pressure." "I willingly perform tasks that appear humiliating."

It's a very simple test, but it cuts close to the bone, doesn't it? It soon makes you wonder if you're really abiding in Christ and loving others and bearing the fruit of the Spirit. "The fruits are the payoff," says Pastor Frazee. "The way to judge a Christian is to see if the power of the gospel is really being lived out."[1]

It's the way to judge a church too, isn't it? Because that is what Jesus was trying to say to the disciples. His commandments were simple. They reached to the very depths of human life and emotions and were capable of transforming the world. But because they were simple, they are sometimes easy to overlook, even among those of us who want so badly to follow him and be the church he intended us to be.

The world is undergoing some very radical changes, and the church must obviously change with it. We don't know—no one can say—what the church of the twenty-first century will finally look like. But we do know, if it is being faithful to Christ, that these will be its most important marks: It will abide in him, as he abides in us. It will be a place of great, unselfish love, based on the love he has already shown us. And it will be a community where the fruits of the Spirit abound—love and joy and peace and patience and kindness and generosity and faithfulness and gentleness and self-control.

And I can promise you one thing: A church with these three qualifications will never die.

God won't let it.

Jesus won't let it.

And other people won't let it.

Lord of the Waves

Immediately he made the disciples get into the boat and go on ahead to the other side, while he dismissed the crowds. And after he had dismissed the crowds, he went up the mountain by himself to pray. When evening came, he was there alone, but by this time the boat, battered by the waves, was far from the land, for the wind was against them. And early in the morning he came walking toward them on the sea. But when the disciples saw him walking on the sea, they were terrified, saying, "It is a ghost!" And they cried out in fear. But immediately Jesus spoke to them and said, "Take heart, it is I; do not be afraid."

Peter answered him, "Lord, if it is you, command me to come to you on the water. He said, "Come." So Peter got out of the boat, started walking on the water, and came toward Jesus. But when he noticed the strong wind, he became frightened, and beginning to sink, he cried out, "Lord, save me!" Jesus immediately reached out his hand and caught him, saying to him, "You of little faith, why do you doubt?" When they got into the boat, the wind ceased. And those in the boat worshiped him, saying, "Truly you are the Son of God."

Matthew 14:22-33

I can relate to this text, can't you? Especially the part where the disciples were afraid. If I am totally honest with myself, I have to admit I spent a large part of my life being afraid.

I remember when I was a small boy and my parents went driving on Sunday afternoons. I tended to get carsick, so they left me with a neighbor lady named Mrs. Blackerby. Mrs. Blackerby was a kindly old sweetheart and normally I liked her. But I always had the feeling when I was left behind on Sunday afternoon that my parents were never going to return, and I would have to dwell in her musty old house for the rest of my life. A sick, fearful feeling swept over me the way a clammy fog moves in on a sunny landscape.

I was a terribly nearsighted boy and was afraid to tell anyone I couldn't see well. I thought I must be defective, and didn't want the fact to be known. When the nurses and ophthalmologists came to our classrooms in the early grades, I always managed to leave and go to the bathroom until they were gone, so they wouldn't discover my problem. I made it all the way into the fifth grade before a sharp-eyed principal spotted my difficulty and I had to start wearing glasses.

As a teenager I was afraid to ask a girl for a date because I knew no girl that I wanted to go out with would want to go out with me. When I would start to speak to one of the prettier or more popular girls in my class my throat always closed up and I had to excuse myself and go away.

When I became a minister I was afraid of disappointing the people I preached to. I'm still afraid of that. If I stop to think about it, my mind seizes up and I can't get on with my sermon.

I am even afraid of retirement. What if I don't like being retired? What if I get out there and I'm bored or don't have enough money to live on or my wife doesn't like having me at home all the time? Is it like going on a cruise? If I get out there and don't like it, is it too late to return?

You see what I mean. Life is full of fears, isn't it? Most of us go through our years afraid of more things than we can count—afraid we won't be liked, afraid we won't be successful, afraid we'll be poor parents, afraid we'll get to the end of the way and look back and realize we've taken the wrong road.

What is that saying, "You know you're getting older when you get to the top of the ladder and find out it's propped against the wrong wall"?

And our fears have a very practical effect on our lives. They keep us from living as freely and openly and happily as we would if we didn't have them. Let me put it even more strongly: Our fears actually inhibit us from doing miraculous things with our lives.

Isn't that the point about Simon Peter in this story? Until he became afraid, Peter could walk on water. "Lord, if that's you," he said, "bid me to come to you." And Jesus bade and he came. But when his fears overtook him, when he saw the fierceness of the waves and realized what he was doing, he promptly sank. He was doing something miraculous until he became self-conscious and lost his confidence. Then he was lost!

Think about your own situation, and how your fears paralyze you or prevent you from doing your best. Maybe you're afraid of forming a new relationship with someone because some of the relationships you've had in the past haven't turned out well. "That other person is really nice," you think, "or appears to be. But I don't know. I've been burned before."

You may be afraid to let go of the job you've got and go out and get another. You remember how hard it is to get oriented in a new position or how embarrassed you were when you lost that good job once before. "I don't like what I'm doing," you think, "but at least it's safe. I think I'll stick it out where I am."

Maybe there's even something very special you think God has wanted you to do with your life and you would like to do it if you only had the courage, but you realize it would be risky to do it now, at your age and with your educational background and everything, so you rationalize. You say, "Well, if God ever makes it *really* plain to me, so that this feeling is something I can't ignore, I'll do it then."

You see? Fear is the great inhibitor.

This is a hard time we live in, isn't it? And here we are about to enter a new millennium.

Our scripture knows how we feel—as if we were in a tiny little boat out on a vast and stormy sea, with the waves bouncing everywhere and tossing the boat around like a leaf or a chip of wood. That little boat was being "beaten by the waves," and the disciples had "the wind against them." Not just the wind, but a gale. It was a violent, threatening night, and the disciples, though they were veterans of the sea, were afraid.

Some friends of mine once took a boat ride on the Sea of Galilee. They were on a large tourist vessel. When they set out, they said, the sky was clear and the sea was calm. But an hour later the clouds came over and the sea began to pitch. Then the rains broke and the waves rose up around them. People were hurled from one side of the boat to the other by the fierceness of the pitching. The captain radioed for helicopters in case the boat capsized. "It was terrible," my friends said; "we were scared to death!"

Ah, but isn't life sometimes like that? Life gets to pitching that way. Like now, with all the changes taking place. Going into a new century and a new millennium when we didn't understand or deal well with the old one. People have changed. Cities have changed. Work has changed. Music has changed. Morality has changed. Expectations have changed. Sometimes it seems as if *everything* has changed.

Even church has changed, hasn't it?

When we were young, church was always the same. We knew what to expect when we attended. Everything was traditional and predictable. Now there are all the new liturgies and all the new music. The preachers don't even sound the same anymore. And the issues are certainly different from the ones we remember in our childhoods—women in ministry, homosexuality, the new morality. You can't go to church today and escape from the world. We keep thinking about that line from Marc Connally's play *Green Pastures,* "Everything nailed down is comin' loose!" It's not just coming loose today, it's flying around as if it were caught in a tornado!

It makes us afraid to leave the old century behind and enter a new one. If the old one was so upsetting, what will the new one be like?

Fears, fears, fears. They dominate our lives, don't they, so we can't live joyously and productively, so that every time we start to walk on water or do something miraculous we end up nearly drowning.

But that's only the negative part of our text, the part that holds a mirror up to our fears and apprehensions. There's a positive side too. In fact, that's what the text is really about.

You see, this text is what the biblical scholars like to call a "post-resurrection" narrative. It's a story about Jesus and the disciples *after* the resurrection, inserted back into the tale of Jesus' earthly ministry. The Gospel writers weren't biographers of the sort we have today. They didn't write everything in sequence. The stories about Jesus calming the sea when the disciples were about to perish—this one and the one in Mark 4:35-41—were written from the perspective of Jesus' triumph over death. The disciples were the early Christians, and the boat itself was a symbol of the church. (If it helps, remember that the Latin word *navis*—"boat"—is the word from which we derive our word "nave" for the center aisle of the church.) The early church was often caught up in storms and found itself perishing. There were times when it seemed highly unlikely that it could survive. But on every one of those occasions Christ rose to the occasion—pun intended!—and saved it. He made the winds and the waves obey him.

We don't know if the stories really happened or if they

were only parables told to remind Christians of the power of God. Either way, their authors must have had in mind the many times in the book of Psalms when the psalmists described God as being Lord of the waves. Here for example is Psalm 93:

> The LORD is king, he is robed in
>   majesty;
>   the LORD is robed, he is girded
>   with strength.
> He has established the world; it
>   shall never be moved;
>   your throne is established
>   from of old;
>   you are from everlasting.
> The floods have lifted up,
>   O LORD,
>   the floods have lifted up their
>   voice;
>   the floods lift up their roaring.
> More majestic than the thunders
>   of mighty waters,
>   more majestic than the
>   waves of the sea,
>   majestic on high is the LORD!
>   (Psalm 93:1-4)

Do you see the extraordinary depth of our text in the light of this? It is not simply a miracle story. It is a story about everyday life—about all the times when the winds blow and the waves beat against our boats and we feel threatened and afraid because of the circumstances. It is a story about now, as we prepare to enter a new millennium and feel awkward and fearful about what we may encounter.

What it says is that there is never a night so dark or a storm so terrible that Christ is not there to help us through, not there to rescue us and make the storm go away.

How does it happen? What are we supposed to do when our fears get hold of us and stop us from living miraculously, the way we ought to?

The answer is really quite simple. It all has to do with where our attention is focused. If it is on our fears, then we will be paralyzed. But if it's on something else—on the Christ of the resurrection—then we will feel empowered and emboldened and everything will be different.

Let me illustrate it in a very simple way. When my wife and I were teenagers and I was courting her, I had to pass a large graveyard to get to her house. It was a very spooky place, as most graveyards are at night. When I would go by, I looked straight ahead, but my peripheral vision was continually straining to catch any sign of movement among the bushes or tombstones. My heart was in my throat from fear and apprehension. But once I had seen my sweetheart and spent an hour or two in her presence, and maybe been rewarded by a little kiss on the front porch as I was leaving, I went past that same graveyard with an entirely different attitude. I was no longer thinking about ghosts and goblins. Now my heart was pounding with love, and that was taking all my adrenaline. I didn't have any left over for being afraid.

This is the way it is when our hearts are fixed on Christ. Then we don't have to worry about fears and foibles. We don't have to face the future with apprehension. We don't have to worry about how things will turn out, because we know that "all things work together for good for those who love God, who are called according to his purpose" (Romans 8:28). We don't have to be concerned about the winds and the waves, and we won't sink into the depths the way Simon Peter did. If we merely keep our eyes upon Jesus, as the old chorus reminded us, everything will be all right.

What was it Jesus said to the disciples? "Take heart, it is I; do not be afraid." "It is I," in the Greek words that lie behind the English translation, is *ego eimi.* Those are the very same words used in the Greek version of the Old Testament when God spoke to Moses at the burning bush and Moses wanted to know God's name. God said, "*Ego eimi*"—I am simply who I am.

The early church recognized this connection. They knew that God was with them in the risen Christ. And they knew that whenever the waves beat against their boats and the waves threatened to destroy them without mercy, the risen Christ would be with them, telling them to have courage and not be afraid.

This is what the story says to us as well. We can stop being afraid and start living a miraculous existence, because the Lord of the waves is with us. That's the central message of our faith. And the best time to realize it is right now, when the waves and winds are giving us a hard time.

Try it. Invite Jesus into the boat with you. Do it in your imagination and see what a difference it makes. Think about the worst problems raging around your life, and then ask Jesus to step in with you. It's all different, isn't it? That's what our story says. When Jesus got into the boat with the disciples, the winds stopped. Just like that! And they all worshiped him, it says, and exclaimed, "Truly you are the Son of God!"

Did they ever doubt it?

Did you?

Sermon 5

The God Who Is About to Create

For I am about to create new heavens
*   and a new earth;*
the former things shall not be remembered
*   or come to mind.*
But be glad and rejoice forever
*   in what I am creating;*
for I am about to create Jerusalem as a joy,
*   and its people as a delight.*
I will rejoice in Jerusalem,
*   and delight in my people;*
no more shall the sound of weeping be heard in it,
*   or the cry of distress.*
No more shall there be in it
*   an infant that lives but a few days,*
*   or an old person who does not live out a lifetime;*
for one who dies at a hundred years will be considered a youth,
*   and one who falls short of a hundred will be considered accursed.*
They shall build houses and inhabit them;
*   they shall plant vineyards and eat their fruit.*
They shall not build and another inhabit;
*   they shall not plant and another eat;*
for like the days of a tree shall the days of my people be,
*   and my chosen shall long enjoy the work of their hands.*
They shall not labor in vain,
*   or bear children for calamity;*
for they shall be offspring blessed by the LORD—

and their descendants as well.
Before they call I will answer,
* while they are yet speaking I will hear.*
The wolf and the lamb shall feed together,
* the lion shall eat straw like the ox;*
* but the serpent—its food shall be dust!*
They shall not hurt or destroy
* on all my holy mountain,*
                                    says the LORD.
                              Isaiah 65:17-25

This is a surprising text, isn't it? We thought God had already finished the creation. We read about it in the book of Genesis—how God made a world out of the void that was there, and separated the seas from the land, and set the sun to rule the heavens by day and the moon by night, and fashioned the animals and birds and fishes, and in a flourishing finale shaped a man from the dust and a woman from his rib, and then rested from all the exertion. As one little boy blurted out to his Sunday school teacher, "My daddy says he is just like God after God made the world—he has been tired ever since he made me!"

And then this text comes along and says God is *about to create new heavens and a new earth*—as if God hadn't retired from creating after all, but is still very much in the business! It really puts the lie to that old eighteenth-century notion that the Creator of the world is like a clockmaker who sets all the clockworks into motion and then absents himself to let it operate on its own, doesn't it? On the contrary, God is still up to the divine elbows in making the world and making the people in the world, and hasn't even begun to rest from the task.

This is a very important piece of information to have as we enter a new century and a new millennium, isn't it? It means that everything is still in the workshop. The world and the universe are still being shaped. God is still actively involved in what is happening in history. God still cares about how everything turns out. And God will not abandon us before all God's promises for a kinder, juster, gentler world have been fulfilled, before there are "new heavens and a new earth."

It is easy to think, standing at the watershed of millennia and looking back over the extraordinary achievements of the last thousand years, that the words of the musical *Oklahoma!* were truly prophetic: "Things have gone about as far as they can go." William L. Renfro, founder of the National Millennium Foundation, said in an article in *The Futurist* magazine: "Consider all we have accomplished during this millennium: We established governments based on the consent of the governed. We discovered science, developed medicine, and then created the universities. We proved the world was round and discovered new worlds beyond our horizons. We split the atom and tapped the power of stars. We mastered flight, moved toward the stars, and reached the edge of time and the universe with our minds."[2]

The last century alone has been a whirlwind of creativity and discovery. In a special edition (Newsweek Extra, Winter 1997–1998), *Newsweek* devoted article after article to the explosion of discoveries that changed forever the way we human beings live our lives on earth. The first airplane flight was in 1903, blood transfusions began in 1905, the modern assembly line appeared in 1913, the zipper in 1914, the electric mixer in 1918, frozen foods in 1924, talking movies in 1926, Scotch tape in 1930, nuclear fission in 1945, the credit card in 1950, color television in 1951, heart transplants in 1967. We put astronauts on the moon in 1969, produced the personal computer in 1975, and developed fiber-optic communications in 1977. We had the World Wide Web in 1990, the Pentium processor in 1993, and the cloning of an adult mammal in 1997.

Many of us have lived through an extravaganza of inventions and discoveries. It is as if the world were a gigantic science fair and important new developments were popping up around us all the time. Things have occurred so rapidly that a popular sociologist named Alvin Toffler coined the phrase "future shock." Our world changes so swiftly today, he said, that we haven't time to absorb one wave of discovery before we are bowled over by another. So we live in a state of perpetual shock and amazement.

But William L. Renfro concludes the list of our great achievements of the last thousand years by asking, "If this past be prologue, what dreams can the Third Millennium hold?"[3] What dreams indeed await realization in the century ahead, not to mention an entire millennium?

Bill Gates, the computer impresario, is already talking about *tactons*, little electrical impulses in clothing we shall don that will send tiny stimuli all over our bodies to transmit pre-programmed experiences, so that we won't just see virtual reality with our eyes and hear it with our ears but experience it in our very nervous systems. Something called the Human Genome Project has set a target date of the year 2010 for producing a molecular blueprint for a human being—an exact sequence of the four chemical letters that make up each of our 80,000 genes and the precise locations of these genes on the twenty-three pairs of chromosomes, which will eventually enable doctors to discover exactly what is wrong with us in an illness and treat it immediately. And the "hottest" area of physical research today, we are told, is in nanotechnology, the science that studies the atomic structure of matter with the intention of using "nanobots," tiny engineering molecules, to rearrange atoms and create virtually anything out of the commonest substances available. Everything we need to exist, it is theorized, from houses and food to vehicles and fuel, can be fashioned out of a few cents' worth of ordinary elements, once we have the technology to do it.

I don't know how you feel about it, but it appears to me

that God is already very much at work creating a new heaven and a new earth. It is occurring all around us all the time. Unfortunately, we don't always give God credit for it. In fact, quite the opposite usually occurs. The more we discover, the more we congratulate ourselves for being clever and ingenious and the less we think about God. Philosophers of science say this is a natural tendency. We have always conceived of God as presiding over the great mysteries of existence, and whenever we have discovered how things work we have removed them from God's territorial supervision and placed them under our own. Thus thunder and lightning once compelled people to bow down in terror before the Almighty, and now that we understand what produces them we merely avoid standing under a tree during a storm. So God is left being a mere "God of the gaps," as Michael Polanyi expressed it, and the gap is constantly being reduced as we learn more about the universe.

This is why it is so important, from a perspective of truth and wholeness, that we hear the voices of the great theoretical physicists of our time, people like Einstein and Oppenheimer and Hawking, who endlessly marvel at the existence and behavior of matter in the universe. They are like Job, the ancient sufferer, who after assuming he knew all there was to know about God had a more direct encounter with the Holy and exclaimed, "I have talked about things that were beyond me, things I didn't really understand! I thought I knew you because I had heard about you and assumed I comprehended who you are, but now I have really seen you in action and it makes me despise myself for my presumptuousness" (Job 42:3-6, paraphrased).

The truth is, we don't really make or create anything on our own. All we do, for all our knowledge and inventiveness, is discover what God has already created and is continuing to create. If our ears were properly attuned to the music of the universe, it would probably sound to us like Handel's

"Hallelujah Chorus," for it would hymn the majesty and creativity of God—and not just of God, but of God *at work!*

What were the initials Johann Sebastian Bach inscribed in the corner of his manuscripts when he had just completed another masterpiece? *S.D.G.*—for *Soli deo gloria.* "To God alone be the glory!" Bach understood. We are not the makers or creators of anything. We only discover, like little children at an Easter-egg hunt, the surprises God has enfolded in the universe. God is the creator, the *only* real creator, of everything that is, and our cleverest scientists are merely adept at unraveling the clues to divine mysteries.

Entering a new millennium, we are like climbers who can stand at the brow of the mountain and gaze in two directions—back to the way the human race has come in the last few thousand years and forward to the way it will be going. It is a wonderful opportunity to embrace a new spirituality for the new age, to bow down before the God who makes everything and confess our great amazement. If we don't, then we enter the new era with blindness and arrogance, claiming for humanity the glory that really belongs to the Creator.

But let's go back to our text for a minute, and remember what Isaiah's representation of the voice of God was saying about the new creation:

> Be glad and rejoice forever
>   in what I am creating;
> for I am about to create Jerusalem as a joy,
>   and its people as a delight.
>   (Isaiah 65:18)

The crux of God's creative attention, the real center of the divine interest, is not finally in what we know as the wonders of nature, which are constantly being discovered and harnessed for our physical welfare. It is in *people.* It is in *human beings.* It is in *us.* "Jerusalem as a joy, and its people as a delight."

143

Does this suggest that we, not the world around us, not all of the marvels and intricacies of nature, are God's greatest challenge as a creator?

We do appear to have given God the most trouble, haven't we? We are the ones who claim the territories that really belong to the Creator and fight over them, aren't we? We are the ones who despoil the earth, paving its surface and polluting its air and streams and soil in the vanity that we are somehow enriched by doing so. We are the ones who choose up sides and threaten to destroy everything on the basis of skin pigmentation and religious beliefs and cultural traditions. We are the ones who think our inventions are really ours and bravely posture as if we would take the place of God.

What was it Paul said in his letter to the Romans? "Ever since the creation of the world (God's) eternal power and divine nature, invisible though they are, have been understood and seen through the things he has made." But people "became futile in their thinking, and their senseless minds were darkened. Claiming to be wise, they became fools; and they exchanged the glory of the immortal God for images resembling a mortal human being or birds or four-footed animals or reptiles" (Romans 1:20-23). That is, they worshiped themselves and other creatures in the world instead of the Holy One who had made them.

God's promise in Isaiah is that God isn't only working on the world, God is working on us, so that the people inhabiting the world will be different. God says there won't be any sound of weeping in the new Jerusalem, and there won't be any children born to live only a few days. People will live to be more than a century in age, and their houses and lands won't be overrun by others. They will enjoy the work of their hands and take pleasure in their families. They will perceive God's answers even before they call upon the divine. The wolf and the lamb and the lion and the ox will feed together in peace. Only the serpent—the symbol of evil and wickedness in the world—will find life difficult, feeding upon the dust of the earth. "They shall not hurt or destroy on all my holy mountain, says the LORD" (Isaiah 65:25).

Ah, you say, all of that language is very nice, but isn't it about the *heavenly* Jerusalem, the one described in the book of Revelation as the final resting place of the saints? It isn't really about life on this earth.

Isn't it? That isn't made clear in the book of Isaiah. In Isaiah, God is speaking as if the promise will be a reality *in this world*, as if all of these wonderful things will come to pass *here* and not in some existence yet to come.

Is it beyond all dreaming? We've spoken of the wonderful inventions and discoveries that have been made in the physical world of the last millennium. But what of all the discoveries in the personal or spiritual worlds? Think of the great insights of the mystics in the Middle Ages. Think of the humanists and reformers, and the birth of the university system. Think of the origin of hospitals and psychiatric wards and rehabilitation centers, of charitable organizations and Alcoholics Anonymous and other helping groups too numerous to mention. Think of the League of Nations and the United Nations and the growing efforts to bring peace and prosperity to the entire world. Think of great personality models such as Francis of Assisi and Clara Barton and Gandhi and Schweitzer and Mother Teresa, and of the power of television to broadcast their lives and messages into homes around the world. Think of the great hunger we have seen in recent years for a new spirituality, one that transcends not only materialism and escapism, but former religious and ideological boundaries as well.

Evil is deeply entrenched in the world, and often expresses itself in terrible ways. In this century alone we have witnessed devastating world wars, the great Holocaust of the Jews, and shocking forms of terrorism. But that shouldn't blind us to the great strides in humanitarianism that have been achieved, and to the democratization of the great ideals of love and acceptance and generosity deriving from our religious heritage. The world may be getting worse and worse, as the power to do wicked things is increased, but it may also be getting better and better, through the love and goodwill and commitment of those who truly care about the rule of God in human affairs.

Whatever we believe about the locus of the new Jerusalem, though—whether here on earth or in a spiritual world to come—we shouldn't fail to glorify God not only for the beauty and intricacy and profligacy of the physical creation around us but for the joy and possibility of the spiritual life opening up inside us.

A friend of mine wrote recently: "I did not know, twenty years ago, that I could experience such wonderful insights into the presence of God in the world of my immediate senses and impressions. I thought I was spiritual then; or at least I tried to be. But my perceptions and revelations then were as nothing compared to the grand transports of the spirit I experience today. Sometimes I feel as if my very being will explode with joy and passion for the universe, God has put it in my heart so strongly to love everything that he has made!"

We don't know what another millennium will bring in the development of science and technology—surely marvels beyond our imagining. Nor can we begin to predict what it will mean in terms of the developing psyche and spirit of humankind—perhaps advances in personal understanding and world government that will make the text in Isaiah seem entirely realizable here on earth.

But whatever it brings, we know it can only enhance our sense of appreciation for the enormous might and intelligence of our Creator. And we know we would all do well to live through the coming years with the letters *S.D.G.* engraved upon our foreheads, reminding us every day that we live, *Soli deo gloria*—"To God alone be the glory!"

Life Beyond Measure

*He looked up and saw rich people putting their gifts into the trea-
sury; he also saw a poor widow put in two small copper coins. He
said, "Truly I tell you, this poor widow has put in more than all of
them; for all of them have contributed out of their abundance, but
she out of her poverty has put in all she had to live on."*

Luke 21:1-4

The countdown is on. Every day now we see or hear some
new reference to the year 2000 that is almost upon us.
Journalists in Britain are fond of calling it "Y2K"—the year
2000. Computer experts are scrambling to convert computer counting systems to the third millennium, so that everything doesn't begin malfunctioning the minute we pass
midnight at the end of the old millennium. Planning com-
missions are busy dreaming up fabulous ways of transition-
ing from one era to another. People are already projecting
where they will be and what they will be doing when the
clock ushers in a new century. Bob Whittock, who manages
an antique store and b&b in Stow-on-the-Wold in the
English Cotswolds, hopes to take his wife, Carol, on a cruise
to the Antarctic, where he served in the British navy as a
young man. They intend to be on a ship sitting in Lockroy
Harbor, where his ship was anchored nearly half a century

ago. Other folks will be on the Concord, buzzing around the world counter-clockwise in order to celebrate the arrival of the new year in all the different time zones.

Novelist Ursula LeGuin, in an article in *Parabola* magazine, wants to know what all the hullabaloo is about. After all, she says, time is only an arbitrary construct—something we invented—and midnight on December 31, 1999, is a mere vanishing point, a moment in a long succession of moments, without any actual dimensions of its own. The real year, she says, lies in its "cyclicalness," in the seasons and in the movements of the earth among the stars, not in some random instant that happens to fall at the end of a thousand years.

She is right, of course. But we are the measurers—human inchworms who go around putting our tapes and calipers on things. We like to dice things up, to divide them into segments, so that we can handle them and maybe even understand them better. And we're getting better and better at it. Now we've invented *nanotechnology*—methods of dividing things into billionths. *Billionths* of seconds and *billionths* of degrees and *billionths* of centimeters.

The problem with all this, from the standpoint of real living, is that we start living by measurements. We can't turn off our passion for taking the measure of everything. We begin measuring things that weren't meant to be measured and worrying when the figures don't tally the way we think they should.

Like: "My work load is bigger than hers but she makes more money than I do." "I'm as smart as he is and he's already a second vice-president of the company." "I've written more books and articles than she has and I'm still only an assistant professor." "We've been married longer than they have and they live in a bigger house than we do." "After all I've done for him, this is the thanks I get."

You see?

Daniel T. Niles, a wonderful preacher I knew years ago from the island of Sri Lanka, said his children were always measuring their bananas. They had banana trees growing in their yard, and every morning his wife would put a banana by each of their plates. They could have all the bananas they wanted. But invariably they held up their bananas to compare their length, and the one with the shortest banana always fussed about it.

I thought that was childish and silly until one day at the dinner table I saw our two sons holding up their forks to see if one was longer than the other.

We are measurers. We instinctively want to lay a ruler down by everything we have and everything everybody else has, and we are unhappy if ours is smaller or cheaper or less impressive than theirs.

And one of the things we measure most, in a society as filled with busyness and pressure as ours, is time. It is no wonder we are conscious of entering a new millennium, because we live by the calendar and the clock. Business people especially. You know how you can tell an executive notebook from an ordinary notebook? It isn't divided merely into days, it's divided into quarter-hours! I suppose if it were the notebook of the CEO of IBM or General Motors, it would be divided into five-minute segments, or maybe even one-minute segments.

It's a damnable thing, isn't it? I remember how guilty I felt when I was on a trip to Africa and having a wonderful time and realized I was counting down the days until I returned home. Imagine! I was slicing up that extraordinary trip, one of the finest experiences of my life, like a loaf of bread or a roll of bologna.

Somewhere in my notebooks I have a saying I wrote down from the lips of one of my African seminary students: "God gave Africans time; God gave Americans watches." There is a big difference, isn't there, between time and watches. Yet we can't seem to help ourselves.

Maybe this is why Jesus appears to have been so fond of the poor widow who cast the two coins into the temple treasury. She was poor—she didn't have much—but she wasn't stopping to count. She wasn't like the Pharisees, who tithed mint and cumin, measuring out exactly how much of their possessions they would give to the Lord. And she wasn't like us, running a regular check on our investments and dividends and pension plans. She was so filled with simple faith, so much in awe of the God of the universe, that she didn't bother to count anymore. She responded with her heart to the wonder of things, not with her head to the size of them.

Wouldn't you like to be that way?

I recall a fellow I knew years ago who scrimped and saved and took a trip to the Bahamas. He said the sky was pure blue and the temperature was seventy degrees. The water was clean and fragrant and his hotel was comfortable. He went down to the beach and thought, "This is living!" He looked around and saw everybody sitting on comfortable beach chairs, and he thought, "That looks relaxing. I wish I had a beach chair. I wonder where they got them." About that time, a man came along renting beach chairs. "How much?" asked the man. "Fifty cents," said the man with the chairs. "That's too high," said the man. "For fifty cents, I can sit on my towel, the way I intended to." But when the man got home he thought back to that moment and said, "That was a crazy decision. There I had spent a small fortune to get to the islands, and was quibbling over fifty cents for a beach chair. It just didn't make sense."

A lot of things don't make sense that way, do they? I mean, we spend too much time measuring what things cost and how big they are and whether we're being treated fairly, when the world is big and bright and beautiful and we should be living in awe every moment that we draw our breath.

The widow in our text stood in such joy and respect before the wonders of life that she opened her hand and dropped all the coins she had into the treasury box in the temple. "Here, Lord, it's all I have." It was a fitting response to the magnitude and the beauty of her existence. She was living, in her quiet, unpretentious way, where Charles Dickens' Scrooge was living after he had his conversion—after he had been with the ghosts of Christmas Past, Christmas Present, and Christmas Yet to Come. Before, he measured everything. Afterwards, he didn't stop to count the cost. Before, everything was done tightly, grudgingly, reluctantly. Afterwards, lightly, loosely, joyously. And as Scrooge characterized the change in himself in the Albert Finney musical version of the story, "I love life!"

We are talking about a religious response to life, aren't we? A spiritual response. Measuring everything, being careful and grudging, is a sign of fear and finickiness, of excessive care and self-interest. We want to be sure we are adequately compensated, that we get what is coming to us, that life doesn't treat us unfairly. But when our spirits are converted, when we see the world in technicolor and realize that it all belongs to God and God is a graceful, lavishing parent, the care and the measuring go out the window. Suddenly life is large and beautiful, and we want to sing and dance and squander ourselves for the sake of others. The distinction between "mine" and "yours" disappears and everything becomes "ours." We don't have to spend our time measuring anymore or worrying about justice, because we are so happy to be alive in such a place and such an hour that we simply want to celebrate!

This is why St. John gives us the description of heaven he provides in the book of Revelation. He pictures an angel measuring the celestial home with a golden rod. "The city lies foursquare," he says, "its length the same as its width; and he measured the city with his rod, fifteen hundred miles; its length and width and height are equal" (Revelation

21:16). Does that sound like us, measuring things? He was accommodating our passion for such matters. But fifteen hundred miles! That distance is greater than the length of the Mediterranean basin, the known world in John's day. It was as much as a man could travel in a hundred days. And not only that, but the city was a *cube*, as high as it was broad and long. That's impossible, isn't it? But in ancient times the cube was considered the perfect form. It was all John's way of saying that heaven is beyond earthly measurement: it is too generous and well proportioned to fit within the way we measure things.

And why is that? Because in heaven *God is all in all*. God's throne is at the center of everything. All people do is praise God. All the angels do is praise God. Worship, adoration, celebration—these constitute everything. And when you're worshiping and adoring and celebrating, you're not worrying about anything else. Life is so immediate and so intense that there isn't thought or care for other things. The present moment of joy has become everything. Life has become so wonderful that it is beyond all measure.

And who is to say things can't be that way for us now? We don't have to wait for heaven. Converted people, people living in the spirit, have a sense of heaven in this life. The widow who gave her two coins did. Heaven lay all about her. She didn't need anything else. She wasn't aware of anything else. Life for her, like heaven in John's description, was perfect, beyond all measure.

The year 2000 is a great milestone in the history of the world. Of course reaching it will affect us psychologically. Even the people who feign little interest in it will be affected. But the more spiritual we are—the more we are caught up in the glory and grandeur of God—the less it will matter to us. Measuring things is for this world. Enjoying them is for the world of the spirit.

Ursula LeGuin, the novelist I mentioned, wrote a science-fiction story called *The Left Hand of Darkness*. For the people in that story, every year is the year one, for that is where all life is focused. They count the years in the past as one-ago, two-ago, three-ago, and so on. What LeGuin was trying to do, she says, is "to catch the idea that *every* year is the year one: it starts fresh, and the numbers attached to it are arbitrary."

Maybe that's the way it ought to be for us. Every year ought to be the most important, and we ought not to need the spur of a new millennium to excite us and make us think deeply about the meaning of life. Right now is the most important moment of our lives, for it is the only one we have. "Today," says the ancient text, "if you hear his voice, do not harden your hearts" (Hebrews 3:15). This is the hour of our salvation, the time for us to realize that life is beyond measure.

Prayer: The years and the centuries are yours, O God; and so are the earth and all space, and life and all power. Thank you for letting us live and play and work in them. And grant that we may be always mindful of your Lordship, in order that we may sing and dance and celebrate in the present moment. Through Christ our Savior. Amen.

Notes

1. The End of the First Millennium

1. George Lincoln Burr, "The Year 1000," *The American Historical Review* 6, no. 3 (April 1901): 437.

2. Popular Emotions as the Millennium Approaches

1. William Ecenbarger, "Here Comes the Millennium!" *Reader's Digest* (October 1996): 76-9.
2. Bruce Handy, "Turn-Off of the Century," *Time*, 5 May 1997, 105.
3. Brian E. Daley, "Judgment Day or Jubilee? Approaching the Millennium," *America*, 31 May 1997, 20.
4. "Point of No Return: An Interview with Ursula K. LeGuin," *Parabola* 23, no. 1 (Spring 1998): 20.
5. Alec Wilkinson, "Millennial Malaise," *The New Yorker*, 13 January 1997, 27.
6. Peter C. Newman, "The Dawn of a New Millennium," *Maclean's*, 30 December 1996/6 January 1997, 49.
7. Jerry Adler, "Fast and Furious Fun," *Newsweek*, 27 January 1997, 71.

3. Great Biblical Themes That Find Resonance in the Approach of a New Millennium

1. Robert N. Bellah et al., *Habits of the Heart: Individualism and Commitment in American Life* (New York: Harper & Row Perennial Library, 1986), 143.
2. Louise Davis, "The Garden of Eden or Doomsday?" *The Nashville Tennessean*, 21 March 1971.
3. Walter Brueggemann, *Finally Comes the Poet: Daring Speech for Proclamation* (Minneapolis: Augsburg Fortress, 1989), 13.
4. William L. Renfro, "A World Future Celebration," *The Futurist*, March-April 1995, 28.

4. The Spiritual Life of the Minister at the Turn of the Millennium

1. Adam Rogers and David A. Kaplan, "Get Ready for Nanotechnology," *Newsweek Extra: 2000: The Power of Invention*, Winter 1997–98, 52.

2. Michael Mayne, *This Sunrise of Wonder* (London: Fount Paperbacks, 1995), 172-73.
3. David Steindl-Rast, *Gratefulness, the Heart of Prayer* (New York: Paulist Press, 1984), 81.
4. R. D. Laing, *The Politics of Experience* (New York: Pantheon Books, 1967), 14.

5. Sermons for a New Millennium

1. Christine Wicker, "Spiritual Fitness: Self-Test Measures Progress and Christian Virtues," *Birmingham News*, 8 November 1996, 3H.
2. William L. Renfro, "A World Future Celebration," *The Futurist*, March-April 1995, 28.
3. Ibid.

A Bibliography of Writings for Preaching on the New Millennium

I. On the history of the first millennium

Burr, George Lincoln. "The Year 1000." *The American Historical Review* 6 (April 1901): 429-39.

Collins, Roger. *Early Medieval Europe, 300–1000.* New York: St. Martin's Press, 1991.

Coulton, G. G. *Life in the Middle Ages.* New York: Macmillan, 1931.

Erdoes, Richard. *A.D. 1000: Living on the Brink of Apocalypse: A History of the Tenth Century for Those Who Hope to See the Year 2000.* San Francisco: Harper and Row, 1989.

Howard, Philip. "The Sense of Our Sensibility: Twenty Words That Define the Twentieth Century." *Times* (London), 14 March 1998, 7.

Hulme, Edward Maslin. *The Middle Ages.* New York: Henry Holt and Co., 1929.

Thompson, James Westfall. *An Economic and Social History of the Middle Ages.* New York: Century Publishers, 1928.

II. On the approach of a new millennium

Angeli, Michael. "The End of the World As We Know It." *Los Angeles,* January 1997, 46-51.

"Beyond 2000: America in the 21st Century." *Newsweek,* 27 January 1997, 48-88.

Bloom, Harold. *Omens of Millennium: The Gnosis of Angels, Dreams, and Resurrection.* New York: Putnam, 1996.

Briggs, Asa. "The March of Time." *History Today,* November 1996, 5-7.

Champion, Sarah, ed. *Disco 2000.* London: Sceptre Press, 1998. [Ten British writers imagine what the end of the century will be like.]

Charbeneau, Travis. "Living in 'Apocutopia'." *The Futurist,* January–February 1993, 60.

Ecenbarger, William. "Here Comes the Millennium!" *Reader's Digest*, October 1996, 76-79.

Hamilton, Kendall, and Steve Rhodes. "What the Stars Say: Floods, Sex, and Bette Midler." *Newsweek*, 23 June 1997, 23.

Handy, Bruce. "Turn-Off of the Century." *Time*, 5 May 1997, 105.

"The Millennium: 100 Events That Changed the World." *Life*, Fall 1997, 12-133.

"Millennium Meditations." *The Futurist*, May–June 1993, 44.

Newman, Peter C. "The Dawn of a New Millennium." *Maclean's*, 30 December 1996/ 6 January 1997, 48-53.

Newsweek Extra: 2000: The Power of Invention. Winter 1997–1998.

Parabola: Myth, Tradition, and the Search for Meaning 23 (Spring 1998). [Entire issue devoted to writings about the new millennium.]

Renfro, William L. "A World Future Celebration." *The Futurist*, March–April 1995, 28.

Savage, M. T. "Dawn of a New Millennium." *Ad Astra*, July–August 1995, 40-43.

Schwartz, Hillel. *Century's End: An Orientation Manual for Futurists*. New York: Doubleday and Co., 1996.

Schwartz, Hillel. "Fin-de-siecle Fantasies." *The New Republic*, 30 July–6 August 1990, 22-25.

Weigel, George. "Comes the Millennium." *Commentary*, March 1996, 46-50.

Wilkinson, Alec. "Millennial Malaise." *The New Yorker*, 13 January 1997, 27.

Yourdon, Edward, and Jennifer Yourdon. *Time Bomb 2000: What the Year 2000 Computer Crisis Means to You!* Upper Saddle River, N.J.: Prentice-Hall, 1997.

III. On the church as it faces the new millennium

Anderson, Leith. *A Church for the 21st Century*. Minneapolis: Bethany House Publishers, 1992.

Daley, Brian E. "Judgment Day or Jubilee? Approaching the Millennium." *America*, 31 May 1997, 8-21.

Reese, Thomas J. "2001 and Beyond: Preparing the Church for the Next Millennium." *America*, 21-28 June 1997, 10-18.

Wuthnow, Robert. *Christianity in the Twenty-First Century: Reflections on the Challenges Ahead.* New York: Oxford University Press, 1993.

IV. On the minister's spirituality in the new millennium

Bell, Martin. *Street Singing and Preaching: A Book of New Psalms.* Nashville: Abingdon Press, 1991.

Buechner, Frederick. *The Sacred Journey: A Memoir of Early Days.* San Francisco: Harper and Row, 1982.

Jones, W. Paul. *The Province Beyond the River: The Diary of a Protestant at a Trappist Monastery.* Nashville: Upper Room Books, 1986.

Killinger, John. *Bread for the Wilderness, Wine for the Journey: The Miracle of Prayer and Meditation.* Rev. ed. Centreville, Va.: Angel Books, 1996.

Mayne, Michael. *This Sunrise of Wonder.* London: Fount Paperbacks, 1995.

Nicholl, Donald. *Holiness.* New York: Seabury Press, 1981.

Nouwen, Henri J. M. *Creative Ministry.* New York: Doubleday Image Books, 1978.

Paulsell, William O. *Rules for Prayer* New York: Paulist Press, 1993.

Rupp, Joyce. *Praying Our Goodbyes.* Notre Dame, Ind.: Ave Maria Press, 1988.

Steindl-Rast, David. *Gratefulness, the Heart of Prayer: An Approach to Life in Fullness.* New York: Paulist Press, 1984.

Wiederkehr, Macrina. *A Tree Full of Angels: Seeing the Holy in the Ordinary.* San Francisco: HarperSanFrancisco, 1988.